THE
LUMBEE

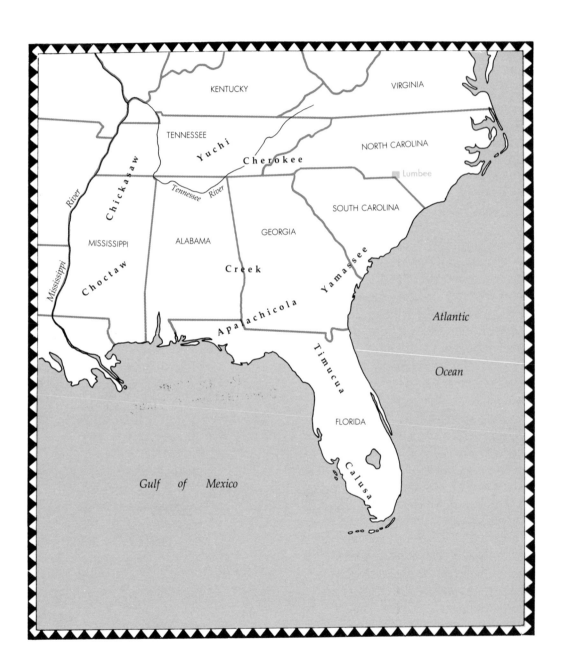

INDIANS OF NORTH AMERICA

THE
LUMBEE

Adolph L. Dial
Pembroke State University, Pembroke, North Carolina

Frank W. Porter III
General Editor

CHELSEA HOUSE PUBLISHERS
New York   Philadelphia

On the cover A 20th-century Lumbee quilt made by a
descendant of Henry Berry Lowrie

Chelsea House Publishers
Editor-in-Chief Richard S. Papale
Executive Managing Editor Karyn Gullen Browne
Copy Chief Philip Koslow
Picture Editor Adrian G. Allen
Art Director Nora Wertz
Manufacturing Director Gerald Levine
Systems Manager Lindsey Ottman
Production Coordinator Marie Claire Cebrián-Ume

Indians of North America
Senior Editor Sean Dolan

Staff for **THE LUMBEE**
Editorial Assistant Nicole Greenblatt
Senior Designer Rae Grant
Picture Researcher Nisa Rauschenberg

First Printing

1 3 5 7 9 8 6 4 2

Library of Congress Cataloging-in-Publication Data

Dial, Adolf L., 1922–
The Lumbee—southeast/Adolf L. Dial.
   p.   cm.
ISBN 1-55546-713-X
      0-7910-0386-8 (pbk.)
1. Lumbee Indians—Juvenile literature. I. Title.
E99.C91D5 1993   92-28917
973′.0975—dc20   CIP

CONTENTS

INDIANS OF NORTH AMERICA

CHELSEA HOUSE PUBLISHERS

INDIANS OF NORTH AMERICA: CONFLICT AND SURVIVAL

Frank W. Porter III

The Indians survived our open intention of wiping them out, and since the tide turned they have even weathered our good intentions toward them, which can be much more deadly.

John Steinbeck
America and Americans

When Europeans first reached the North American continent, they found hundreds of tribes occupying a vast and rich country. The newcomers quickly recognized the wealth of natural resources. They were not, however, so quick or willing to recognize the spiritual, cultural, and intellectual riches of the people they called Indians.

The Indians of North America examines the problems that develop when people with different cultures come together. For American Indians, the consequences of their interaction with non-Indian people have been both productive and tragic. The Europeans believed they had "discovered" a "New World," but their religious bigotry, cultural bias, and materialistic world view kept them from appreciating and understanding the people who lived in it. All too often they attempted to change the way of life of the indigenous people. The Spanish conquistadores wanted the Indians as a source of labor. The Christian missionaries, many of whom were English, viewed them as potential converts. French traders and trappers used the Indians as a means to obtain pelts. As Francis Parkman, the 19th-century historian, stated, "Spanish civilization crushed the Indian; English civilization scorned and neglected him; French civilization embraced and cherished him."

Nearly 500 years later, many people think of American Indians as curious vestiges of a distant past, waging a futile war to survive in a Space Age society. Even today, our understanding of the history and culture of American Indians is too often derived from unsympathetic, culturally biased, and inaccurate reports. The American Indian, described and portrayed in thousands of movies, television programs, books, articles, and government studies, has either been raised to the status of the "noble savage" or disparaged as the "wild Indian" who resisted the westward expansion of the American frontier.

7

Where in this popular view are the real Indians, the human beings and communities whose ancestors can be traced back to ice-age hunters? Where are the creative and indomitable people whose sophisticated technologies used the natural resources to ensure their survival, whose military skill might even have prevented European settlement of North America if not for devastating epidemics and the disruption of the ecology? Where are the men and women who are today diligently struggling to assert their legal rights and express once again the value of their heritage?

The various Indian tribes of North America, like people everywhere, have a history that includes population expansion, adaptation to a range of regional environments, trade across wide networks, internal strife, and warfare. This was the reality. Europeans justified their conquests, however, by creating a mythical image of the New World and its native people. In this myth, the New World was a virgin land, waiting for the Europeans. The arrival of Christopher Columbus ended a timeless primitiveness for the original inhabitants.

Also part of this myth was the debate over the origins of the American Indians. Fantastic and diverse answers were proposed by the early explorers, missionaries, and settlers. Some thought that the Indians were descended from the Ten Lost Tribes of Israel, others that they were descended from inhabitants of the lost continent of Atlantis. One writer suggested that the Indians had reached North America in another Noah's ark.

A later myth, perpetrated by many historians, focused on the relentless persecution during the past five centuries until only a scattering of these "primitive" people remained to be herded onto reservations. This view fails to chronicle the overt and covert ways in which the Indians successfully coped with the intruders.

All of these myths presented one-sided interpretations that ignored the complexity of European and American events and policies. All left serious questions unanswered. What were the origins of the American Indians? Where did they come from? How and when did they get to the New World? What was their life—their culture—really like?

In the late 1800s, anthropologists and archaeologists in the Smithsonian Institution's newly created Bureau of American Ethnology in Washington, D. C., began to study scientifically the history and culture of the Indians of North America. They were motivated by an honest belief that the Indians were on the verge of extinction and that along with them would vanish their languages, religious beliefs, technology, myths, and legends. These men and women went out to visit, study, and record data from as many Indian communities as possible before this information was forever lost.

By this time there was a new myth in the national consciousness. American Indians existed as figures in the American past. They had performed a historical mission. They had challenged white settlers who trekked across the continent. Once conquered, however, they were supposed to accept graciously the way of life of their conquerors.

The reality again was different. American Indians resisted both actively and passively. They refused to lose their unique identity, to be assimilated into white society. Many whites viewed the Indians not only as members of a conquered nation but also as "inferior" and "unequal." The rights of the Indians could be expanded, contracted, or modified as the conquerors saw fit. In every generation, white society asked itself what to do with the American Indians. Their answers have resulted in the twists and turns of federal Indian policy.

There were two general approaches. One way was to raise the Indians to a "higher level" by "civilizing" them. Zealous missionaries considered it their Christian duty to elevate the Indian through conversion and scanty education. The other approach was to ignore the Indians until they disappeared under pressure from the ever-expanding white society. The myth of the "vanishing Indian" gave stronger support to the latter option, helping to justify the taking of the Indians' land.

Prior to the end of the 18th century, there was no national policy on Indians simply because the American nation had not yet come into existence. American Indians similarly did not possess a political or social unity with which to confront the various Europeans. They were not homogeneous. Rather, they were loosely formed bands and tribes, speaking nearly 300 languages and thousands of dialects. The collective identity felt by Indians today is a result of their common experiences of defeat and/or mistreatment at the hands of whites.

During the colonial period, the British crown did not have a coordinated policy toward the Indians of North America. Specific tribes (most notably the Iroquois and the Cherokee) became military and political pawns used by both the crown and the individual colonies. The success of the American Revolution brought no immediate change. When the United States acquired new territory from France and Mexico in the early 19th century, the federal government wanted to open this land to settlement by homesteaders. But the Indian tribes that lived on this land had signed treaties with European governments assuring their title to the land. Now the United States assumed legal responsibility for honoring these treaties.

At first, President Thomas Jefferson believed that the Louisiana Purchase contained sufficient land for both the Indians and the white population.

Within a generation, though, it became clear that the Indians would not be allowed to remain. In the 1830s the federal government began to coerce the eastern tribes to sign treaties agreeing to relinquish their ancestral land and move west of the Mississippi River. Whenever these negotiations failed, President Andrew Jackson used the military to remove the Indians. The southeastern tribes, promised food and transportation during their removal to the West, were instead forced to walk the "Trail of Tears." More than 4,000 men, women, and children died during this forced march. The "removal policy" was successful in opening the land to homesteaders, but it created enormous hardships for the Indians.

By 1871 most of the tribes in the United States had signed treaties ceding most or all of their ancestral land in exchange for reservations and welfare. The treaty terms were intended to bind both parties for all time. But in the General Allotment Act of 1887, the federal government changed its policy again. Now the goal was to make tribal members into individual landowners and farmers, encouraging their absorption into white society. This policy was advantageous to whites who were eager to acquire Indian land, but it proved disastrous for the Indians. One hundred thirty-eight million acres of reservation land were subdivided into tracts of 160, 80, or as little as 40 acres, and allotted to tribe members on an individual basis. Land owned in this way was said to have "trust status" and could not be sold. But the surplus land—all Indian land not allotted to individuals— was opened (for sale) to white settlers. Ultimately, more than 90 million acres of land were taken from the Indians by legal and illegal means.

The resulting loss of land was a catastrophe for the Indians. It was necessary to make it illegal for Indians to sell their land to non-Indians. The Indian Reorganization Act of 1934 officially ended the allotment period. Tribes that voted to accept the provisions of this act were reorganized, and an effort was made to purchase land within preexisting reservations to restore an adequate land base.

Ten years later, in 1944, federal Indian policy again shifted. Now the federal government wanted to get out of the "Indian business." In 1953 an act of Congress named specific tribes whose trust status was to be ended "at the earliest possible time." This new law enabled the United States to end unilaterally, whether the Indians wished it or not, the special status that protected the land in Indian tribal reservations. In the 1950s federal Indian policy was to transfer federal responsibility and jurisdiction to state governments, encourage the physical relocation of Indian peoples from reservations to urban areas, and hasten the termination, or extinction, of tribes.

Between 1954 and 1962 Congress passed specific laws authorizing the termination of more than 100 tribal groups. The stated purpose of the termination policy was to ensure the full and complete integration of Indians into American society. However, there is a less benign way to interpret this legislation. Even as termination was being discussed in Congress, 133 separate bills were introduced to permit the transfer of trust land ownership from Indians to non-Indians.

With the Johnson administration in the 1960s the federal government began to reject termination. In the 1970s yet another Indian policy emerged. Known as "self-determination," it favored keeping the protective role of the federal government while increasing tribal participation in, and control of, important areas of local government. In 1983 President Reagan, in a policy statement on Indian affairs, restated the unique "government to government" relationship of the United States with the Indians. However, federal programs since then have moved toward transferring Indian affairs to individual states, which have long desired to gain control of Indian land and resources.

As long as American Indians retain power, land, and resources that are coveted by the states and the federal government, there will continue to be a "clash of cultures," and the issues will be contested in the courts, Congress, the White House, and even in the international human rights community. To give all Americans a greater comprehension of the issues and conflicts involving American Indians today is a major goal of this series. These issues are not easily understood, nor can these conflicts be readily resolved. The study of North American Indian history and culture is a necessary and important step toward that comprehension. All Americans must learn the history of the relations between the Indians and the federal government, recognize the unique legal status of the Indians, and understand the heritage and cultures of the Indians of North America.

Mrs. Josephine Smith, a Lumbee, poses in front of her tobacco barn. Throughout their recorded history, most Lumbee have earned their livelihood as farmers, with tobacco as one of their primary crops.

WHO ARE THE LUMBEE?

In 1709, John Lawson made a trip through the English colony of Carolina. As the surveyor general of the colony, he needed to know all about the lay of the land and the people who inhabited it. Lawson's travels took him northeast, from the settlement of Charleston, located on a peninsula near where the Ashley and Cooper rivers flow into the Atlantic Ocean in present-day South Carolina, to the vicinity of the Neuse River in what is now central North Carolina. The lands he traveled through were thickly forested and well watered, still only sparsely settled by English-speaking settlers. The most numerous human inhabitants, by far, were the various Native American peoples who lived there.

In the course of his journey, Lawson passed through the territories of many Indian peoples, including the Catawba, the Tuscarora, and the Coree. He learned as much as possible from each group about how they lived, and he recorded his findings about their ways of life in a book he wrote about his journey entitled *History of Carolina*. Soon, Lawson came to believe he probably knew more about Indian customs than any other white man in Carolina; indeed, he has been called the "first North Carolina historian."

As Lawson made his way east toward the Atlantic coast, he met a group of Indians who challenged everything he had learned. In a section of *History of Carolina* entitled "A Description of North-Carolina," Lawson wrote about his experience with the "Hatteras Indians" who "either then lived on Roanoke Island, or much frequented it." (Roanoke is a small—36-square-miles—island located off the northeast coast of present-day North Carolina between Pamlico and Albemarle sounds, just

The first English settlers arrive at Roanoke Island in 1585. Many Lumbees share family names and possibly ancestry with the lost Roanoke Island colonists.

east of Dare County.) To a greater extent than any other Indians he had encountered, the Hatteras were extremely friendly, especially to Englishmen: "They value themselves extremely for their Affinity to the English," wrote Lawson, "and are ready to do them all friendly Offices." They were also somewhat familiar with the ways of whites. For instance, the Hatteras knew that the English could "talk in a book" (read) and "make paper speak" (write). Their appearance was also unusual; Lawson noted that among the Hatteras gray eyes were not uncommon, which was not the case with the other Indian peoples he had known.

The Hatteras had their own explanation for why they were so different from other Indian peoples. They told Lawson that several of their distant ancestors had been whites, from whom they had inherited certain physical and cultural traits. The Hatteras' story led Lawson to formulate a theory that scholars have been debating ever since—the notion that these Indians were descendants of the English settlers of the "lost" colony of Roanoke.

More than 100 years earlier, Sir Walter Raleigh—soldier, poet, historian, and courtier—had sent 117 men, women, and children across the Atlantic Ocean to establish a colony on the

An engraving made from John White's watercolor of Native American fishing methods. White's paintings constitute the earliest European visual documentation of Native American life in present-day North Carolina and Virginia.

coast of what is now North Carolina. The English then called this region, as well as the seaboard north of it, Virginia, in honor of the putative chastity of the unmarried queen of England, Elizabeth I, who had given Raleigh a charter that allowed him to take possession of land in North America in her name. Spain and France had already claimed huge parts of the Americas as colonies—Spain in present-day Mexico, Central America, South America, and the American Southwest; and France along the St. Lawrence River and in the Great Lakes region—and England was looking for suitable lands with which to begin its own American empire. The Spanish had realized significant profits by extracting gold and silver from American mines, and Raleigh and his colonists hoped that Virginia would prove as rich.

The colonists were led by the artist John White, who had already visited North America at least twice; once as a member of Martin Frobisher's unsuccessful second expedition in quest of the Northwest Passage and once as part of an earlier, unsuccessful effort to colonize *Roanoke Island*. White had achieved some small renown for the drawings and paintings he made on his earlier visits to America, and after the settlers arrived on Roanoke in the summer of 1587, he set about compiling a visual chronicle of the endeavor. His watercolors emphasized the natural bounty of the colonists' new home, with its vast array of plants and animals unfamiliar to the newcomers. They re-

corded also the Englishman's impressions of the nearby Indian population, which demonstrated the contrast between the settlers' ill-fated attempts at survival in a strange land and the more prosperous way of life of the Native Americans. White's famous painting of Secoton, an Indian village southwest of Roanoke near the Pamlico River, for example, shows more than a dozen multifamily dwellings and several fields ripe with corn.

The English colonists, meanwhile, had arrived too late in the season to plant crops, and they had failed to bring enough livestock and provisions to carry them through the winter. After less than two months, accordingly, White was dispatched back to England to persuade Raleigh to send the necessary supplies. Though no one knows for certain what befell the colonists in the months before White returned, presumably they experienced a significant degree of hunger, as had those of their countrymen who had attempted to settle Roanoke Island just two years earlier. Indeed, those earlier settlers had proved so unable to cope with their new environment that they would have starved had it not been for the largesse of their Indian neighbors, who brought them food, planted several fields of corn for them, and attempted to show them how to spear and trap fish; even so, hunger was the major cause of their abandoning Roanoke within a year.

White arrived in England from Roanoke in November 1587. He hoped, of course, to persuade Raleigh to send

The only clue to the fate of the disappeared settlers of the Roanoke colony was the word Croa-toan *carved into a fence post of the colony's stockade (a tree trunk in this somewhat stylized depiction of the arrival of the relief ships from England.)*

a supply expedition immediately, but England was then preparing for the attack of the "invincible" Spanish Armada—a seaborne invasion of the island organized by King Philip II of Spain for the purpose of restoring England to Catholicism under his sway and ending the frequent attacks of English pirates on his shipping and American outposts. Virtually every En-glish ship was being requisitioned for the kingdom's defense, and White and Raleigh found it difficult to organize a relief expedition. Once, Raleigh was able to put together a fleet of seven or eight ships, only to have them claimed for the defense forces at the last moment. Another time, White actually sailed for Roanoke with two ships, but the two vessels were beset by French privateers on the high seas and looted. White was wounded in the attack; for these and perhaps other, unknown reasons, he did not return to Roanoke until mid-August 1590, almost exactly three years after he had left the fledgling colony.

He found the colony utterly deserted, the cabins and stockade overgrown with weeds and pumpkin vines. Footprints were visible, and assorted possessions of the colonists were scattered about. On a tree trunk the carved letters C R O were legible; the word CROATOAN had been notched, "in fair capital letters" according to White, on a fence post of the stockade.

Though the fate of the Roanoke colonists is regarded as one of the greatest mysteries in American history, White was not perplexed by the cryptic messages that were the only clues left about what had become of his fellow settlers. He and the other colonists had come to agree that Roanoke Island was not an ideal site for a settlement; if, while he was gone, the colonists were forced to move as a result of "great distress," they would so designate to White by carving a Maltese cross on some visible object. The absence of such an indicator cheered White, as did his understanding of what the carved words meant: the colonists, for whatever reason, had gone to *Croatoan*, an island south of Roanoke that was the home of Manteo and his people, Indians who had been exceedingly friendly to the English. Though White was able to search only briefly and unsuccessfully for his miss-

ing compatriots, he was, he wrote, nevertheless "greatly joyed that I had safely found a certain token of their being at Croatoan," believing that this indicated that they were safe.

In the years that followed, other English settlers and explorers tried to find the Roanoke colonists. Although to date no conclusive evidence regarding their fate has been discovered, some secondhand reports suggest that White's conclusions were correct. For instance, Captain John Smith, founder of the first permanent English settlement in North America at Jamestown, Virginia, wrote in 1608 that the region's Indians claimed that there were people living along the Roanoke River who dressed like Englishmen. William Strachey, an early settler of the Virginia colony, wrote in 1613 that according to the local Indians, the Roanoke colonists had merged with a local people and subsequently moved inland, where they constructed and lived in two-story stone houses more like European dwellings than Native American habitations.

Decades later, several white travelers, including Lawson, recorded meeting Indians familiar with European customs in what is now Robeson County in south-central North Carolina. One adventurer, a German immigrant named John Lederer who claimed to have rambled through much of unsettled North Carolina in the 1670s, wrote of hearing about a "powerful nation of bearded men," which struck him as odd since "the Indians never have any,

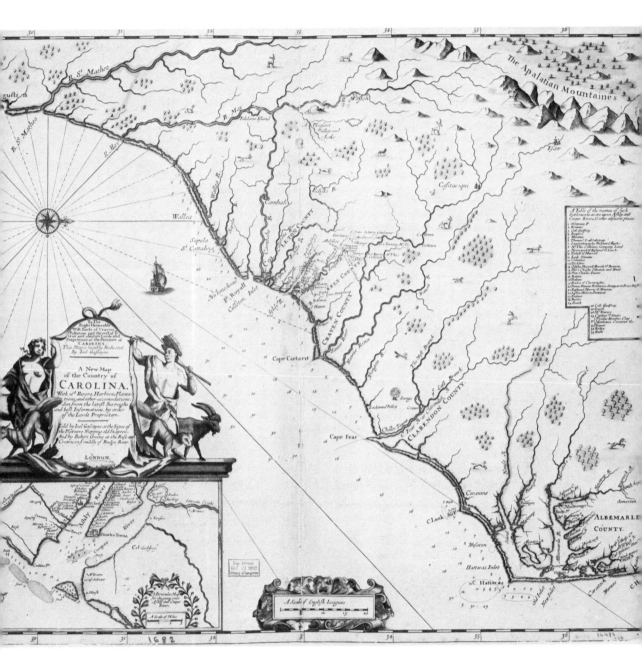

A 1682 map of North Carolina, oriented with east at bottom and north to the right. Roanoke Island (designated Roenoque I. on this chart) is at lower right, just inside the barrier at the mouth of the Albemarle River. The new homeland of the Lumbee was to the west of the Cape Fear River.

it being a universal custom among them to prevent their growth by plucking the young hair out by the roots." A minister, the Reverend Morgan Jones, claimed to have been traveling in the vicinity of what is now Robeson County in the 1660s when he was captured by Indians who spoke English. According to Hamilton McMillan, a late-19th-century North Carolina historian and state legislator, when European settlers finally reached the Lumber River in the 1730s—the Lumber flows southeast through the heart of present-day Robeson County—they found a "large tribe of Indians, *speaking English*, tilling the soil, owning slaves and practicing many of the arts of civilized life." McMillan concluded that the Roanoke colonists had in fact merged with Manteo's people and moved to Robeson County. Among other points, he cited as evidence that 41 of the 95 surnames of the colonists were held by Robeson County Indians. He also discovered that "the traditions of every family bearing the name of one of the lost colonists point to Roanoke Island as the home of their ancestors."

In 1891, historian Stephen Weeks published an article in the *Papers of the American Historical Association* that offered still more evidence that the Robeson County Indians were descended from English settlers. Weeks maintained that the distinctive dialect spoken by the Robeson County Indians was closely related, in several key matters of pronunciation, usage, and idiom, to the English language as it was

spoken in Elizabethan England. The peculiarities of the dialect suggested to Weeks that it had been learned from the Roanoke Island colonists and passed down over the centuries. No convincing alternative explanation has been advanced as to how the Robeson County Indians learned to speak English in such a fashion, for evidence indicates

The Lumber River (Lumbee River in native dialect) gave the Indians of Robeson County the name by which they are known today.

that the Indians were already speaking their dialect when the first European settlers reached the Lumber River in the 1700s, and most of these were Scottish highlanders who spoke Gaelic as their primary language.

Despite the persuasiveness of these arguments, many historians and scholars have remained skeptical about the lost colony theory. One group of people, however, has never doubted the theory's validity—the Indians

A Lumbee family in 1948. Standing from left at rear are Ralph Brooks, his wife Lovedy Lock-lear, and their son Silas Brooks; in front are Sarah and Lawrence Brooks. Although the debate about the origins of the Lumbee persists, the Lumbee themselves have never doubted that they are an Indian people.

of Robeson County. Now known as the Lumbee, they trust and respect the old stories of their origins that have been passed on from parent to child for centuries.

The Lumbee are also certain of another truth that others have been prone to doubt—that they are an Indian people. Because of their ancestry, the Lumbee adopted certain ways of white society long before their Indian neigh-bors did. Unlike most other tribes, the Lumbee have lost or forgotten the language and many other aspects of their ancestral culture. In the eyes of many non-Indians, the Lumbee consequently appear to be less "Indian" than some other groups.

Historically, the Lumbee have found the U.S. and North Carolina governments especially hard to convince that they are indeed a distinct Indian people. For more than 100 years, the Lumbee have battled to have their Indianness recognized and to receive from the state and federal governments all the benefits and privileges to which they are entitled by right of their identity as Native Americans. Their persistence and the governments' confusion are reflected in the number of names by which the Lumbee have been labeled. The Indians of Robeson County have been officially known as the Lumbee only since 1953. (The name is derived from the Lumber River, which was sometimes referred to as the Lumbee River.) Previously, the Lumbee have been officially designated as the Croatan Indians of Robeson County (1885), the Indians of Robeson County (1911), and the Cherokee Indians of Robeson County (1913). (The Cherokee appellation reflects the theory, for which there is also some basis in Lumbee oral tradition, that the Lumbee are descended from the Cherokee. Other theories and traditions also cite possible descent, as the result of various historical circumstances, from Eastern Siouan peoples and the Tuscarora of the Iroquoian linguistic family. In all likelihood today's Lumbee are descended, in varying degrees, from all or some of these peoples as well as from the lost colonists.)

The Lumbee's greatest victory in their fight for recognition occurred in 1956, when an act of the U.S. Congress confirmed that the Lumbee were in fact Indians. The triumph was more symbolic than substantive, however, for the legislation also stated that "nothing in this act shall make [the Lumbee] eligible for any services performed by the United States for Indians because of their status as Indians." Providing such services for the Lumbee would have cost the government about $100 million per year. But the Lumbee have always, of necessity, exhibited a great degree of self-sufficiency; it is this characteristic, more than any other, that has allowed them to maintain their identity as a people, and it is this trait that enables them to continue their struggle, for despite past setbacks, the Lumbee remain determined to achieve full recognition and equal rights—as Indians and as Americans. They refuse to accept others' narrow definitions of "Indianness." They know that the way a person looks or behaves does not make him or her a Lumbee. Instead, they know that their Indianness lies in what they share—a love of their Robeson County home, a special history and heritage, and perhaps most important, a certain way of viewing the world born from their unique past. ▲

The many swamps of Robeson County provided the Lumbee with a natural barrier against their enemies.

ESTABLISHING
AN
IDENTITY

There are no written records that tell us when the Lumbee first came to Robeson County. The only source of information is the Lumbee's oral tradition—that is, the stories about their history that have been passed down by word of mouth through many generations—as well as the secondhand accounts of a handful of outsiders who had heard of or claimed to have made some contact with the Lumbee.

According to their own tradition, the Lumbee first moved inland from the coast to what is now Sampson County, which is in the south-central part of North Carolina. They then traveled southwest into present-day *Robeson County*, where they probably arrived by about 1650. The precise reason for their migration is unknown, although several reasons suggest themselves. As an Indian people who had adopted non-Indian ways, the Lumbee were in a peculiar situation, and they probably

did not feel comfortable among their Indian neighbors. In addition, the time period in which the Lumbee migration likely occurred was one of no small amount of upheaval and population dislocation in the Carolinas. Significant numbers of white settlers were beginning to enter the North Carolina region from Virginia, resulting in a disruption of some of the native populations; many tribes migrated to remove themselves from the path of white settlement. These tendencies became even more pronounced in the decades after 1650, when diseases introduced by the European newcomers began to devastate native populations and warfare between whites and Indians—most notably the Tuscarora War of 1711–13—and among different Indian peoples resulted in even greater movement.

Whatever the reason for their migration, the Lumbee found a haven—for a time—in Robeson County. In the

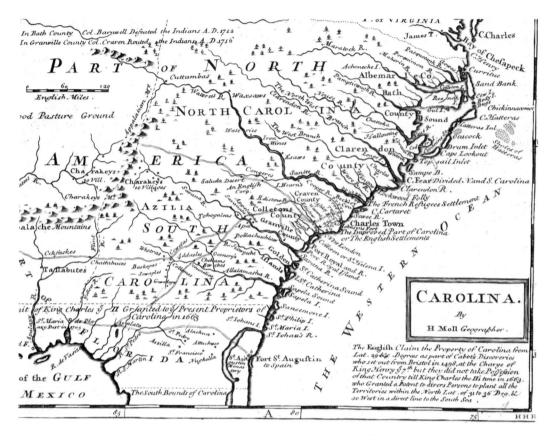

This map of the Carolinas was drawn in 1728, just a few years before the beginning of extensive white settlement in the vicinity of the Lumbee homeland.

17th century, the region was removed from the path of both white and Indian settlement and protected by natural barriers. Robeson County is ridden with swamps, negotiable only by the initiated and even then with great caution, and at the time was heavily forested. Even the Lumber River itself constituted a kind of barrier: a 20th-century Lumbee described it as an "old, winding, treacherous, dangerous, devious river," and on its upper reaches it is still sometimes referred to, as it has

been throughout the period of human settlement along its banks, as Drowning Creek. In addition to protection, the rich natural environment of Robeson County provided the Lumbee with sustenance. An abundance of game animals lived in its forests, numerous fish swam in its rivers, and the well-watered land was fertile.

The Lumbee's isolation, however, was not to last. By the late 17th century, significant non-Indian settlements had been established along Albemarle

Sound, which is just north of Roanoke Island, and at Charles Town, which is now the city of Charleston, South Carolina. The Lumbee's lands lay directly between these settlements, and in the ensuing decades white settlers began moving north and south until, ultimately, they reached south-central North Carolina and Lumbee territory. Huguenot (French Protestant) settlers, having fled religious persecution in their homeland, came to South Carolina in large numbers in the late 16th century; by the 1700s, they had reached the Pee Dee River, southwest of the Lumber, and likely had some contact with the Lumbee. During the Tuscarora War, according to Lumbee tradition, a North Carolina militia and its Indian allies, many of them Cherokee, marched through Lumbee territory on a trail known later as the Lowrie Road.

But the first great wave of non-Indian settlement in Lumbee territory began in the 1730s with the arrival of Scottish Highlanders in south-central North Carolina, initially along the upper Cape Fear River, in lands recently vacated by the defeated Tuscarora, and then along its tributaries. These newcomers, most of whom spoke Gaelic, soon reached the Lumber River, where, according to Lumbee tradition and the work of historians such as Hamilton McMillan, they found a tribe of English-speaking Indians already firmly established. According to McMillan, these Indians "occupied the country as far West as the Pee Dee, but their principal seat was on the Lumber, extending along that river for twenty miles. They held their lands in common and land titles only became known on the approach of white men."

Though their self-chosen isolation had come to an end, the Lumbee found themselves better suited than many of their Indian neighbors—in a number of unique ways—to adapt and adjust to the coming of European settlement. At various times in the 18th century, several different epidemics of smallpox—just one of many fatal infectious diseases unwittingly introduced to the native peoples of North America by the European conquerors and colonizers—devastated the Indians of the Southeast. Because Native American peoples had no inborn immunity to the diseases brought by the Europeans, such as smallpox and measles, these and other ailments spread incredibly rapidly among the various Indian populations and were often deadly to a much higher degree than among comparable European populations. The Lumbee's English ancestry apparently provided them some degree of immunity, however. Smallpox epidemics in 1738 and 1759, for example, claimed the lives of an estimated half of the Catawba, a powerful tribe whose lands neighbored those of the Lumbee; though the Lumbee were similarly exposed, few fell ill.

The Lumbee were also better equipped than many other Native American peoples to hold on to their land. Like most other Indian peoples in the East, the Lumbee held and worked their lands in common, but they

An early European engraving of a Native American village. The first English settlers in North America tended to regard the cultivation of crops (note the field of corn at upper left near the trees) as an indication of ''civilized'' as opposed to ''savage'' behavior on the part of the Indians.

adapted easily to the European custom of individual land ownership certified by deed or another legal document, adopting the practice as a necessity in the face of white settlement in order to hold on to lands that they had long regarded as their own. Robeson County land ownership records indicate that Lumbees were among the first recipients of land grants in the area. Henry Berry and James Lowrie, who were both Lumbees, received land grants on Lowrie Swamp, east of the Lumber River, from King George II of England in 1732. Lumbees named John Brooks and Robert Lowrie purchased tracts of 1,000 acres and 640 acres, respectively, in 1735 and 1736, and the number of Lumbee deeds to land increased steadily through the rest of the 18th century.

The seeming willingness of the Lumbee to accept the concept of private property, as understood by the European settlers, apparently helped smooth relations between the newcomers and the longer settled. If the interaction between European settlers and Indians in Robeson County was often somewhat short of ideal, it was also, for many years, significantly less bloody than that which prevailed in many other parts of North America. In large part, this was because the Robeson County Indians did not fit the pejorative European definition of "savageness" that white settlers applied to Indian cultures elsewhere. The Lumbee neither looked (in terms of apparel; skin color was another story) nor behaved much differently than the European settlers. They lived in European-style houses, farmed using European-style methods, apparently maintained no tribal structure, wore European-style clothes, readily adopted the European concept of private property, and spoke English rather than a tribal language. In short, they were in many ways much like the new settlers in Robeson County and the other small farmers and landholders who were elsewhere trying to fashion an existence for themselves on the American frontier. The Lumbee way of life was so similar to the settlers' own that whites felt compelled to treat the Indians as more or less equals, as evidenced, for example, in the granting of land deeds to Lumbees. Though not unique, the Lumbee success in gaining patents of land ownership was certainly unusual.

"Lumbee-white relations were generally serene [during the colonial period]" wrote Adolph L. Dial and David Eliades in *The Only Land I Know*, a history of the Lumbee people. "Indeed, with acceptance of the concept of private property, the most visible difference between the Lumbees and their new neighbors was in skin color, not in status or occupation. . . . During the colonial period, since there were no decided cultural differences to set them apart, the Lumbees apparently experienced little discrimination because of their darker hue. Since the colonial definition of an Indian was cultural rather than racial (that is, an Indian was a person with an Indian way of life), the Lumbees' difficulties with the newcomers were essentially economic in nature." That is, the Lumbee competed with the white settlers as farmers and landholders, to occupy and own the most fertile land and wrest a satisfactory living from it. The first federal census of the United States, taken in 1790, recorded the presence of 85 Lumbee families in Robeson County, who were listed under the classification of "all free persons not white"; it is likely that a significant number of other Lumbee families and individuals went uncounted.

Despite the many similarities, it is clear that the Lumbee continued to regard themselves as distinct from the white population. Although the Lumbee accepted the concept of private property as ratified by ownership documents, they were less willing to acknowledge the necessity of paying money to secure ownership of lands on which they had long resided, did not—as did the settlers—necessarily regard formerly communal lands as "vacant" and open for settlement, and they did not believe that their status as free landholders obligated them to service in the colonial militia; and they could be forceful in resisting attempts to impose such viewpoints on them. Thus, in 1754, as the North Carolina colony went about raising a militia to send to the aid of Virginia in its war against its native population, the government agent dispatched to present-day Robeson County (then part of Bladen County) to muster soldiers reported the presence of, on "Drowning Creek [the Lumber

River] . . . fifty families, a mixt crew, a lawless people, possessing the land without patent or paying any quit rents; shot a surveyor for coming to view vacant lands, Quakers [as to] muster or paying."

The "lawless people" referred to were, there is little doubt, the Lumbee. Their being a "mixt [mixed] crew" refers to the uncertainty about their racial ancestry that existed even then; *quitrents* refers to the practice, under the English system of land ownership by which North Carolina was being surveyed and parceled out, of paying fees for the use of land—the payer of the quitrent thereby commuted his obligation to provide military service. Quakers, or Members of the Religious Society of Friends, founded the colony of Pennsylvania and were, by religious belief, dedicated pacifists who refused to bear arms, either as individuals or in government service. The anonymous government agent who penned this report is likening the Lumbee to the Quakers in their opposition to military service, although the Lumbee were apparently not adverse to using violence to prevent coercion or to protect what they regarded as their own lands.

Several Lumbees did serve in the rebellious American forces during the American Revolution, however. Though their motivations for doing so are unknown, presumably they believed, as did the colonists who took up arms, that they would be better off as residents of the independent state of North Carolina than as English colo-

During the American Revolution, several Lumbee fought with the American forces for the cause of independence and were rewarded after the war with land grants and pensions.

nists. The Lumbee service on the victorious American side apparently helped their status in Robeson County; several of those who served were rewarded either with government pensions, land grants, or other property—including black slaves. Some portion of the land and property thus redistributed had been seized from Loyalists (or Tories, as they were also known)—those individuals who had decided to cast their lot with the British during the revolution. In the words of one historian, Robeson County "was the scene of a murderous civil warfare of unparalleled atrocity" between the Loyalists and rebel sympathizers in the closing days of the war, and it is a measure of the social status of the Lumbee at the time that they were allowed to benefit from the seizure of Tory property. After the war, feelings against the Tories con-

Andrew Jackson (at right, on white charger) leads the American forces to victory in December 1815 at the Battle of New Orleans, the final encounter of the War of 1812. Jackson subsequently became a national hero and was eventually (in 1828) elected president of the United States, but to Native Americans he was a villain: a fierce prosecutor of wars against the Creek and the Seminole, Jackson was also the foremost proponent of the Indian removal policy.

tinued to run high, and they were disenfranchised (denied the privilege of voting). Although they were not regarded as white by the non-Indian population of Robeson County, the Lumbee were allowed to vote as freemen nonetheless.

Their status as free citizens apparently disposed the Lumbee to the American cause in the War (again with Great Britain) of 1812, in which several Lumbee served in the American forces at a time when most other Indians who became involved in the conflict pledged their allegiance to the British. With the rapid expansion of American settlement beyond the boundaries of the original 13 colonies and the consequent continued overrunning of tribal lands, most Indians had come to see Americans as their greatest enemies, but their status as landholders and free citizens allowed the Lumbee to take a different position.

The War of 1812 took place at a time when the Indians of the Midwest and Southeast were trying, under the inspired leadership of a Shawnee chief named Tecumseh, to organize themselves into a confederacy to resist continued American expansion into their lands. Tecumseh and his allies sided with the British during the war; though his dream of an Indian confederacy died with him at the Battle of the Thames in 1813, the fear he had instilled in American settlers—of an organized, unified Indian opposition capable of resisting widespread settlement—lived on. That fear, combined with the seemingly insatiable hunger of American settlers for new land, helped motivate the mounting political pressure to remove the Indian peoples of the East from their traditional lands. After years of warfare intended to drive the Indian peoples of the East from their lands, Congress in 1830 passed the *Indian Removal Act*, which gave the president (at the time, Andrew Jackson, who as a military man had earlier led U.S. troops against both the Creek and the Seminole) the right to negotiate with eastern tribes for their relocation (or removal) to land west of the Mississippi. The message behind the act was clear—the United States intended to remove all eastern Indians, by force if necessary, that it considered a threat to the economic and physical well-being of its citizenry. Even those

The modern-day Lumbee artist Gene Locklear painted this portrayal of the Cherokee people in 1838 on the Trail of Tears—their tragic odyssey from their traditional homelands in the southeastern United States across the Mississippi River to present-day Oklahoma.

Indian peoples who had maintained peaceful relations with the United States faced removal so long as they occupied lands coveted by American settlers.

As a nontribal people who owned land as individuals, the Lumbee were not directly affected by the Indian Removal Act, but several of their Indian neighbors experienced the tragedy of removal. The Cherokee perhaps suffered most. During the aptly named Trail of Tears—the Cherokee's forced march, under government supervision, from their southeastern homeland to the new territory assigned them in present-day Oklahoma—half of the tribe's population died from starvation, exhaustion, or disease.

The first Indian removals took place at a time of increased attention to the politics of race and color in the South. In 1822, a purported uprising of slaves and free blacks, allegedly led by a free mulatto named Denmark Vesey, was uncovered in its "planning" stages in Charleston, South Carolina, and repressed with great force; 37 of the alleged conspirators were hanged. Nine years later, a black man named Nat Turner led a bloody revolt of nearly 100 of his fellow slaves in Virginia. By the time militiamen crushed the rebellion, nearly 60 whites had been killed. One hundred blacks were also killed in the course of the manhunt for the rebels, and Turner and 19 others were captured and hanged. Before these rebellions, whites in the South had spent much time and effort trying to convince

themselves and others that slavery was essentially a paternal, benign system that benefited both whites and blacks. The latter were, the argument continued, content and grateful for the care taken of them, but the uprisings made the self-evident absurdity of such propaganda that much more immediately recognizable and left southern whites fearful and desperate to exert even more stringent control over the region's black population, free and slave. Legislation was introduced forbidding blacks to assemble or circulate after nightfall, and night riders were hired to patrol the roads to enforce the new laws. In every southern state except for Maryland, Kentucky, and Tennessee, whites were prohibited from teaching slaves to read and write.

Action was taken against free blacks as well as slaves. In many sections of the South around this time, free blacks were deprived of the few civil rights they had enjoyed. In North Carolina in 1835, a special state constitutional convention called to address the thorny question of disproportionate representation in the state legislature found time to also consider the matter of suffrage for free blacks. Previously, free black males in North Carolina had been allowed to vote, provided they met certain property-ownership qualifications (the same restrictions applied to white males), but the delegates to the constitutional convention decided that as "this is a nation of white people—its offices, honors, dignities and privileges are alone open to, and to be enjoyed

Nat Turner, the leader of the greatest slave revolt in American history, is surprised by Benjamin Phipps, a poor white farmer, as he emerges from his camouflaged hiding place in Southampton County, Virginia, on October 30, 1831. Turner was the last of the conspirators to be captured; the rebellion he masterminded forced white Americans to reconsider their attitudes regarding slavery and inspired even more stringent racial codes in the South.

by, white people" and that blacks lack "intelligence and moral character," therefore "no free negro, free mulattoe, or free person of mixed blood . . . shall vote." The convention's decision was then ratified by the voting population of the state. Shortly thereafter, free blacks were also deprived of their right to bear arms without a license or to serve in the militia.

At first, the Lumbee were not greatly concerned about either removal or the so-called free Negro codes. Though they may have sympathized with the plight of those tribes who were displaced, they believed that it was those Indians' adherence to traditional ways, rather than their Indian identity itself, that had made their presence intolerable to whites, and they did not immediately believe that their own status would be affected. A similar reaction took place in regard to the free Negro codes: As slave owners themselves, the Lumbee did not initially regard the new legislation as being of especially great consequence to their own way of life.

What the Lumbee did not recognize was that whites' view of the tribe was changing. Previously, whites had categorized Indians on the basis of their behavior. Essentially, an Indian was someone who acted like an Indian, someone who exhibited behavior that whites regarded as typical of an Indian, or "savage." As the government moved toward a policy of removal, however, a new justification was needed, for the tribes that were first slated for relocation west of the Mississippi—the Choctaw, Cherokee, Chickasaw, Creek, and Seminole—had in fact been so successful in adopting new ways of life in the wake of white settlement that they were referred to collectively by whites as the Five Civilized Tribes. Now, however, settlers wanted their land, and a reason was needed to rationalize their removal. Indianness (and by extension

"savagery") was now held to be something inherent or racial, attaching to the color of one's skin rather than to specific behavior or lifeways. All Indians, regardless of their way of life, were now held to be inferior by virtue of the color of their skin and their "Indian blood." Similar reasoning was applied to blacks and to the issue of slavery. As it became increasingly difficult to justify slavery as a benevolent institution, and as political pressure was mounting to limit its expansion into new territories and states and even to force its abolition altogether, its supporters were forced to find justification for it on grounds other than economic convenience or necessity. Thus an increased emphasis was placed on the supposed inferiority—usually in terms of intelligence and character—of blacks as a rationalization for slavery's continued existence. By the logical extension of this racist premise, the rights and freedoms of free blacks, as well as slaves, had to be curtailed, since it was blackness itself—in terms of skin color and ancestry—that rendered its possessor inferior, not his or her social status as a free or enslaved black.

For the Lumbee, the most important consequence of these trends was that all nonwhites were henceforth to be regarded as inferior, and their rights and freedoms were to be curtailed accordingly. Although whites had long acknowledged the Lumbee as Indians, they had made a distinction between the Lumbee and other Native Americans because of their adoption of white ways. Now, despite all that the two peoples shared culturally, whites were coming to regard the Lumbee as very different from them, largely because of the color of their skin. Regardless of their history or position in society, all nonwhites—in Robeson County and elsewhere in the South—were being grouped together. Color was the only thing that mattered, and soon it would mean everything. In a short time in Robeson County, the social classification "free person of color," under which the Lumbee had been grouped for legal purposes, would become synonymous in law and in practice with the classification "free Negro," and all the restrictions aimed at free blacks would also be applied to the Lumbee.

An 1835 court case offered the first indication of the changing legal and social status of the Lumbee. Charles Oxendine, a Lumbee man, pleaded guilty to assaulting another Lumbee and was fined $15. When the judge discovered Oxendine did not have the money to pay his fine, he ordered that the defendant, as a free person of color, be made to work for "any person who will pay the fine for his services for the shortest period of time."

Oxendine was furious. In his eyes, the court was essentially, albeit on a temporary basis, turning him—a legally free man—into a slave. When he appealed the constitutionality of the statute that allowed such discriminatory treatment of nonwhites, the state supreme court avoided ruling on the substance of his issue and local officials

decided to drop the charges against him altogether, but the lesson to the Lumbee remained clear: different rules of justice would now apply for Lumbees and whites. In several subsequent cases, individual Lumbees appealed various cases of discriminatory legal treatment to the state's highest court, most notably several involving legislation that prohibited free persons of color from possessing firearms and other weapons without a license. (In predominantly poor rural communities such as those found in Robeson County at the time, where hunting and fishing provided a significant portion of many individuals' livelihood, such firearms and weapons statutes constituted a significant restriction on behavior. They reflected as well the fear of black rebellion that had been instilled in the white populace.) Although the Lumbee rarely won such cases, their pursuit of appeals to the high courts reveal a sophisticated understanding of the U.S. legal system indicative of their overall adoption of the ways of white society; such adept use of the legal system as a means of defense was often a resort of Indian peoples generally regarded by whites as "civilized," most notably the Cherokee. Indeed, several Lumbees earned a reputation, to the dismay of their white neighbors, for being particularly litigious.

Nevertheless, individual whites in Robeson County did not hesitate to take advantage of the changing legal status of the Lumbee for their own personal gain. Among their most infamous tac-

Though to the whites of Robeson County he was little better than a murderous bandit, Henry Berry Lowrie is revered to this day by the Lumbee as their greatest hero, a Robin Hood–like figure who fought for his people against oppression and injustice.

tics, so far as the Lumbee were concerned, were what became known as *tied mule incidents.* A white farmer would bring his own livestock—a mule, some pigs, and a few cows—onto an Indian's land. The mule would be tied to a post, the cows freed in a pasture with the Indian's own animals, and the pigs put in the pen with the rest of the swine. The unscrupulous farmer would then call in the authorities and claim that the Indian had stolen the animals. Dubious of his prospects for receiving a fair trial, the innocent Lumbee would often agree to work for the farmer or give him some property in exchange for dropping the charges.

Not surprisingly, the economic status of the Lumbee declined with the change in their legal status. According to the 1850 census, only half of the estimated 200 Lumbee families in Robeson County owned real estate. According to Giles Leitch, a white Robeson County attorney who provided testimony about conditions in the region to a congressional committee in 1870, the last slaves owned by the Lumbee had been "sold from them"—presumably a euphemism for taken, by whatever means—by 1840. (White southerners, of course, continued to hold slaves until the end of the Civil War in 1865.) On the eve of the Civil War, most Lumbee men were farmers or unskilled laborers; a much smaller number of others were carpenters, blacksmiths, coopers, shoemakers, bakers, merchants, or millers.

Ultimately, the southern states, including North Carolina, seceded from the Union, banded together as the Confederacy, and then, beginning in 1861 and for the next four years, fought the Civil War to preserve their system of white superiority, of which slavery was the most obvious manifestation. Robeson County's civil war would last far beyond 1865, however, for the cessation of hostilities between the states of the North and the South marked only the beginning of a kind of guerrilla warfare between the white establishment and a band of Lumbee—outlaws to some, Robin Hoods to others—bent on avenging past and present injustices. ▲

THOMAS LOWERY.

ROBESON COUNTY, NORTH CAROLINA.—THE SCENE OF THE BANDITS' OPERATIONS.

CALVIN OXENDINE.

HENRY BERRY LOWERY AND HIS GANG IN THE SWAMP.

RESCUE OF LOWERY'S WIFE AND CHILDREN.

A SHREWD MANŒUVRE.

HENDERSON OXENDINE.

MOSS NECK.

GEORGE APPLEWHITE.

THE NORTH CAROLINA BANDITS.—FROM SKETCHES AND PHOTOGRAPHS BY OUR SPECIAL ARTIST.—[SEE PAGE 251.]

These illustrations of several members of the Lowrie Gang, their environment, and their exploits illustrated a March 30, 1872, article in Harper's Weekly *magazine on the so-called Lowrie War.*

THE LOWRIE WAR

Despite their reduced social status, most Lumbees sided with the Confederacy at the outbreak of the Civil War. Some even joined the Confederate forces, though in general their enlistment was not encouraged. Instead, government authorities in the South sought to use them, against their will, as laborers, alongside black slaves, on the construction of fortifications—most notably Fort Fisher—along the North Carolina coast. This construction was considered essential to the war effort; Fort Fisher was to provide defense for the strategically important city of Wilmington, which served as a supply center for the Southern armies in Virginia and as a critically important harbor for the blockade runners who were challenging the Union's naval stranglehold on the South's harbors. Though the Lumbee were willing to serve in the army, provided their enlistment was of their own free will, they resented being forced into labor, which again made a mockery of their legal definition as freemen by reducing their status to little better than slaves. To make matters worse, conditions in the labor camps were abominable. The work was exhausting and often dangerous, food rations were paltry, medical care was unavailable, and the camps themselves were overcrowded, unsanitary, and unhealthy.

The Lumbee resisted conscription by running away from the camps in large numbers. They took shelter in the familiar swamps of Robeson County, where it was extremely difficult to track them. There, they made contact with Union soldiers who had escaped from Confederate prison camps, some runaway slaves, and other members of their people, who had fled their homes to escape being drafted into labor on the coast. Any favorable sentiment the Lumbee had felt toward the Confederacy was soon exhausted, and many helped the escaped Union prisoners

Elizabeth Harris Dial (right) was the daughter of James Brantly Harris, a bullying Home Guardsman whom the Lumbee regarded as the meanest man in Robeson County. Elizabeth Harris was a girl of 12 when her father was murdered in January 1865, allegedly by Henry Berry Lowrie.

avoid recapture by sheltering them, guiding them through the swamps, and sharing food. Though the bands of Lumbee in the swamps were able to live off the land to a certain extent, they also survived by raiding livestock, often from more prosperous white farmers. Such behavior, combined with the perceived pro-Union sentiment of the Lumbee, enraged their white neighbors, whose response, as the war drew to a close and a Union victory became inevitable, grew increasingly unrestrained and violent.

In this angry climate, a Confederate government official and prominent landowner named James P. Barnes ac-

cused the sons of a prominent Lumbee farmer, Allen Lowrie, of stealing two of Barnes's best hogs. (Allen Lowrie's ancestor, James Lowrie, had been one of the two Lumbees to receive a land grant from King George II in 1732.) Barnes claimed the Lowries had butchered the animals to feed Union runaways and threatened to kill the men if he ever caught them on his farm again. Though the Lowries had been known to befriend Union escapees, no one knows for certain whether they were responsible for the theft of the swine, although it is certain that the churchgoing Allen Lowrie enjoyed an excellent reputation in his community as a farmer and a carpenter and that he was relatively prosperous. Barnes, by contrast, was the object of considerable resentment for his role in enacting conscription in Robeson County.

On December 21, 1864, Barnes himself was shot, from an ambush, in the chest. His attackers—two young Indians, supposedly—emerged from cover and approached the dying man, who begged for mercy. They then shot him in the face. Several neighbors responded to the screams of the dying man, who used his last breath to accuse two of Lowrie's sons, William and Henry Berry, of his murder.

With so many white men away fighting the war, the responsibility for policing Robeson County had been seized by the so-called *Home Guard*, a combination militia and vigilante organization with a reputation among the Lumbee for enforcing various land-grab schemes, such as the infamous tied-mule incidents. As the South's military condition deteriorated, the Home Guard became increasingly vengeful in its behavior toward the Lumbee.

One of the most notorious Home Guardsmen, so far as the Lumbee were concerned, was a huge, ornery bully and bootlegger named James Brantly Harris. Harris, who was considered disreputable even among the whites of Robeson County, took responsibility for policing *Scuffletown*, as the whites tended to refer to Lumbee settlements or gatherings, where he apparently considered his primary duties to be hunting Union prisoners and Lumbee escapees from the labor camps and rounding up other Lumbees for con-

Protected by the guns of Fort Fisher, a Confederate ship prepares to run the Union blockade off Wilmington, North Carolina. Though the blockade was intended by the North to halt all commerce between the Confederacy and foreign powers, Wilmington's protected harbor and strong defenses made it the most important East Coast center for the blockade runners.

scription. He also earned himself a nasty reputation for visiting—usually forcibly—unwanted attention on Lumbee women. "Brant" Harris is remembered in Lumbee legend as "the meanest man in Robeson County."

At some point in late 1864, Harris's attention to a young Lumbee woman angered her boyfriend, who threatened to kill the Home Guardsman. In response, Harris in January 1865 laid a night ambush for his rival and fired from cover, killing him—or so he thought. Closer examination revealed the victim to be another Lumbee, Jarman Lowrie, son of George Lowrie and nephew of Allen Lowrie. The intended victim had been another brother of Allen and George Lowrie.

Although the local authorities had no intention of arresting or trying Harris for Jarman Lowrie's murder, he now had a major problem on his hands, for the large Lowrie clan, as they had demonstrated in the James Barnes affair, protected their own. Harris, for all his swaggering ways, was properly terrified. When Allen and Wesley Lowrie,

Confederate pickets stand guard at Fort Fisher in January 1865, by which time, according to its commander, Colonel William Lamb, the fort constituted the "last gateway between the Confederate States and the outside world." The fort's walls, built in part with conscripted Lumbee labor, were huge mounds of sand, heaped 9 feet high and 25 feet thick.

Jarman's brothers, returned from the labor camps at Fort Fisher on a furlough, Harris, who had originally conscripted them, arrested them for desertion and arranged to personally transport them to the train that would carry them back to the camps. En route, the handcuffed Lowrie brothers were bludgeoned to death. Harris claimed self-defense.

To many of the people of Robeson County, the recent events were a tragedy. The Lowrie brothers' funeral at New Hope Baptist Church was well attended by both Indians and whites, few of whom were left unmoved by the eulogy spoken by their father, George:

> We have always been friends of white
> men. We were a free people long
> before the white men came to our
> land. Our tribe lived in Roanoke in
> Virginia. When the English came in
> our land, we treated them kindly.
> One of our men went to England in
> an English ship and saw the great
> country. There is the white man's
> blood in these veins as well as that of
> the Indian. In order to be great like
> the English we took the white man's
> religion and laws. . . . In the fights
> between the Indians and white men
> we always fought on the side of the
> white men, yet white men treated us
> as Negroes. Here are our young men
> killed by a white man, and we get no
> justice, and that in a land where we
> were always free.

But powerful words would not be enough to restore peace to Robeson County, nor to attain justice for the Lumbee. A warrant was issued for Harris's arrest, but before it could be carried out, Harris was shot to death on January 15, 1865, as he guided his buggy down a Robeson County road. According to Lumbee tradition, his bullet-riddled carcass was then either dumped in an abandoned well or buried hastily in an unmarked grave lying north-south—a sign of profound disrespect on the part of the Lumbee, who honor their dead by laying them to rest lying east-west, facing the sun, the giver of all life.

Though the assassins were never positively identified, most whites and Indians believed the most recent murder to be the work of Henry Berry Lowrie, yet another of Allen Lowrie's sons and a cousin of the slain Jarman Lowrie. The 18-year-old Henry Berry—this Native American outlaw had been born on the Fourth of July in 1847—was among those young Lumbee men who had, initially, taken to the woods and swamps to avoid being conscripted into work in the labor camps (though Henry Berry's flight now had equally as much to do, in all likelihood, with his involvement in the Barnes murder). He was now gathering around his charismatic person a small band of like-minded young men—some only in their teens—motivated by the desire to exact retribution for the long history of white mistreatment of the Lumbee.

Because the elusiveness and woodcraft of Henry Berry Lowrie and his followers kept them beyond the reach of white justice, the Lumbee fully expected that justice to be visited upon

The rubble of the Atlanta railway yard bears testimony to the fury of the Union troops of General William Tecumseh Sherman, who began their bloody march to the sea in that Georgia city in the late autumn of 1864. From Savannah, on the Atlantic coast, Sherman turned his forces back north, and their path then took them through Robeson County.

the larger community, and they took steps accordingly. The collapse of the Confederacy was imminent, increasing the rage of the Lumbee's white neighbors, and the Union general William Tecumseh Sherman had already embarked on his famous March to the Sea through the heartland of the Confederacy. Sherman's intention was to crush the South's will to continue fighting, which he accomplished by destroying as much of its productive capacity—industrial and agricultural—as he could along his bloody path. It was a war against all the people of the South as well as its armies, and the swath Sher-

man's forces cut through the South brought them to Robeson County in March 1865. Several Lumbees allegedly served the Union forces as guides, while others, expecting whites to vent their rage and helplessness on the Lumbee community, took to conducting raids for the purpose of obtaining weapons and supplies. One Lumbee, Hector Oxendine, was executed by the Home Guard for allegedly aiding Sherman's troops.

Inevitably, white vengeance was focused on the Lowrie family. In March 1865, the Home Guard arrested Allen Lowrie and several of his relatives, including his wife, Mary, and three of his sons. The prisoners were taken to a nearby farm belonging to one Robert McKenzie, who had, according to the Lumbee, long coveted the Lowries' lands. At the McKenzie farmstead, 80 white men had gathered to watch the Home Guard punish the Lowrie family. While the female Lowries were locked in a smokehouse, the male Lowries— Allen and his sons William, Calvin, and Sinclair—were questioned at gunpoint on a variety of charges: that they had committed robberies, that stolen property had been found on their land, that they had aided Union prisoners, that they knew of secret stores of weapons kept by other Lumbees, that the Lowrie sons had dodged service in the labor camps. The Lowries denied all the allegations; the stolen property that the white men cited as evidence had been, said the Lumbees, planted on the Lowrie property in a kind of variant on a tied-mule incident. Tiring of interrogation after several hours, the Home Guard selected a "jury" from its ranks, which quickly pronounced all four men guilty, though Sinclair and Calvin Lowrie's punishment was to be less harsh than the rest because the stolen property had been found on land owned and occupied by Allen and William.

Father and son were then taken back to their homestead, forced to watch as a black slave was made to dig their grave, tied to a tree, blindfolded, and executed by a firing squad of 12 men.

This house in the swampy fastnesses of Robeson County was once home to Henry Berry Lowrie, his wife, Rhoda Strong, and their three children, Sally Ann, Nellyann, and Henry Delaware Lowrie.

Watching from the woods in a patch of gallberry bushes, according to Lumbee lore, was Henry Berry Lowrie. His brothers Sinclair and Calvin were then made to accompany the Home Guard in a fruitless search for Union soldiers and weapons caches until, after several days, they were let go with a warning that "if there was any more mischief through that neighborhood they would have to suffer for it, made no difference who did it." Several months later, Sinclair Lowrie and his mother, Mary, were again "arrested" by the Home Guard, this time for supposedly hiding weapons on their property. Mary was tortured by being tied to a tree and blindfolded, as if in preparation for her own execution; guns were then fired over her head, reducing her to a state of nervous collapse. Soon thereafter, Henry Berry Lowrie convened a council of the remaining members of his clan to announce his intention to wage war against the whites of Robeson County. "All of you who wish to join me come along," he is supposed to have said. "You who do not I never want to speak to again."

Over the next several years, the "Lowrie Gang" succeeded in killing or driving from Robeson County all those directly responsible for the murders of Allen and William Lowrie. The gang's core membership consisted of two of Henry Berry's brothers, two cousins, two brothers-in-law, two unrelated Lumbees, two blacks (former slaves), and one white, but it was Henry Berry Lowrie himself who appealed most to

the imagination of his people and became the stuff of Lumbee legend, which has imbued him with almost superhuman qualities. By most accounts phenomenally handsome, unusually intelligent, charismatic, and blessed with superb stamina and strength, Henry Berry Lowrie is supposed to have been able to pick more cotton, cut more wood, and plow more acres than any other man in Robeson County, and there was no man around who could track him down. His appeal to women is often commented on; unlike the loutish Brant Harris, he is said to have always behaved gallantly toward them and to have taken pains to see that they were never physically harmed as the result of his raids.

It was Henry Berry Lowrie's attentiveness to women—specifically, to a single woman—that landed him in jail for the first time. On December 7, 1865, at the Lowrie farmstead, Henry Berry married his 16-year-old cousin Rhoda Strong, the most beautiful girl in the Lumbee community, the "queen of Scuffletown." The postnuptial feasting had just begun when the Home Guard arrived to take the groom away for the murder of James Barnes. Because Sherman's men had burned the jail in Lumberton, the largest town in Robeson County, Lowrie was taken to Whiteville, 30 miles away, for incarceration. The building there proved no more secure, however; the handcuffed Henry Berry became the first man to escape from the Whiteville jail—supposedly through the time-honored method of

The Lowrie Gang on the run in the swamps of Robeson County; an illustration from the 1872 Harper's Weekly *article. Henry Berry Lowrie, said a Robeson County clergymen named Sinclair, "is really one of those remarkable executive spirits that arises now and then in a raw community, without advantages other than nature gave him. He has passions, but no weaknesses, and his eye is on every point at once."*

sawing his way through the bars on his window with a file smuggled to him in a cake by his wife—and made his way successfully back to Scuffletown, where he and his band returned once more to the swamps.

"My band is big enough," Lowrie said about his gang. "They are all true men, and I would not be as safe with more. We mean to live as long as we can, to kill anybody who hunts us, from the Sheriff down, and at last, if we must die, to die game. . . . We are not allowed to get our living peaceably and

we must take it from others." Those whom they took from were invariably white, and the gang is said to have distributed the proceeds among the less fortunate members of the Lumbee community. Initially, the Lowrie gang eschewed violence, except against those who had murdered their leader's kinsmen. Their marauding escalated in intensity after 1867, when a grand jury refused to indict any of the Home Guardsmen in the murders of Allen and William Lowrie and the mistreatment of Mary Lowrie, and especially after 1868, when a new white sheriff formally declared all the members of the band outlaws.

To most in the Lumbee community, the Lowrie Gang were heroes, their defiance and elusiveness a source of pride, their violence and lawlessness a courageous and justified response to oppression, and the outlaws could generally count on sympathy and aid from their people. The white attorney Giles Leitch explained to a congressional committee "that among his [Lowrie's] class and color there is a little pride that we have been unable to take them; that he and his men can conquer and whip all that go after them." Whites generally saw things differently and regarded the Lowries as simple criminals with no claim to a higher purpose: "They seemed to fear nothing, whilst they showed a ferocity, premeditation, and insolence frightful to behold; spreading terror and dismay wherever they saw fit to go; no one not an inhabitant of the county at the time can realize the situation; nearly all of our citizens, with here and there an honorable exception, seemed *terror-stricken*," wrote Mary Norment, whose husband was killed by the gang.

In late 1868, a newly elected sheriff, Benjamin Howell, tried to bring peace to Robeson County. By extending a pledge of safe conduct, he persuaded Henry Berry Lowrie to meet with him and then to surrender, assuring him that in the new court system imposed on the South by the victorious North he would receive a fair trial. Lowrie was

taken to the new county jail in Lumberton, but in a short time various vigilante groups were clamoring that he be turned over to them, and he began to fear for his safety. So, for the second time, he escaped and returned to the comparative safety of the swamps.

Now the so-called Lowrie War began in earnest. The gang turned its attention to Reuben King, the former sheriff, who had been defeated in an election for that office by Howell. Most whites continued to regard King as the rightful officeholder, however, principally because of his forceful law enforcement methods with regard to the county's Indian and black communities, which to the Lowrie gang made him a particularly apt target. The Lowrie band apparently went to King's house intending only to rob him, but a scuffle ensued and the former sheriff was shot to death. In the ensuing months, a new captain of the Police Guard (the postwar successor of the Home Guard), Owen Clinton Norment (husband of Mary Norment), led an intensified effort to bring the outlaws to bay and succeeded in capturing several members of the band, but in March 1870 he was gunned down as he stepped outside his house one evening to investigate a noise. Several weeks later, all the members of the band who had been captured—including two who had been tried, convicted of murder, and sentenced to hang—managed to escape from jail in Lumberton and from an even more secure facility in Wilmington. The state legislature placed a

bounty on Henry Berry Lowrie—
$12,000, dead or alive. The primary
members of the gang would bring their
captors or slayers $6,000 apiece.

Robeson County now descended
into a state of virtual guerrilla warfare.
Over the next three years, 18 people
would become casualties of the Lowrie
War. Vigilantes and bounty hunters executed blacks and Indians suspected of
aiding and abetting the Lowrie Band,
and the gang exacted revenge in kind
and killed its pursuers.

One of the most sensational of these
killings was of a detective from Boston,
Massachusetts, named John Saunders,
who settled in Scuffletown in 1869,
passed himself off as a teacher, slowly
gained the confidence of the Lumbee,
and eventually made contact with
Henry Berry Lowrie. Saunders promised to help the outlaw and his men
escape Robeson County and make a
new life out beyond the Mississippi or
in Mexico. The detective's real plan,
however, was to lure the gang into
South Carolina or Georgia, where, removed from the protection of the
swamps and far from the aid of their
Lumbee friends and relatives, they
could be more easily apprehended.
Saunders would be rewarded, of
course, with a lucrative bounty.

In time, Henry Berry Lowrie learned
that Saunders was in close communi-
cation with his most implacable ene-

The Harper's Weekly *illustration of the Lowrie Gang's rescue of Henry Berry Lowrie's wife, who had been taken into custody by the Robeson County authorities. The engraving consider- ably overdramatizes the incident; in reality just the threat of a confrontation was enough to convince the authorities to release their prisoners.*

mies among the Robeson County whites and was planning to betray him. In November 1870, Lowrie arranged a rendezvous with Saunders and the detective's fellow conspirators in the William McNeill family, and the unsuspecting whites were taken prisoner. While plans were being made to transport Saunders to a swampy hideaway of the gang's known as the Devil's Den, the McNeills were let go with some words of warning from Henry Berry Lowrie:

> God damn you, I have a great mind to kill you right here. I ought to have killed you before. You have been hunting me for years. You are young, stout and healthy; however, I don't want to take your blood. I hate to interfere with you and your people; but you have already done so much to have me hanged or shot that it would be right if I should kill you right here. I will let you go this time, however; but make yourself scarce in this country. . . . You won't know when your time has come.

At the Devil's Den, Saunders was blindfolded, tied to a tree, and executed. According to one member, the band then tried to bury the body as "decently as [they] could" and sent a last letter Saunders had penned off to his family in Boston.

Saunders's fate did little to discourage other bounty hunters. By the spring of 1871, two members of the Lowrie Gang had been caught and killed, one by a bounty hunter as he slept and the other by hanging after a legal arrest and trial. Believing they were on the verge of destroying the band, the Police Guard rounded up the wives of several of the outlaws, including Rhoda Strong Lowrie, and held them for aiding and abetting the gang; essentially, the women were taken as hostages to compel the band's surrender. Henry Berry Lowrie then had a dictated message delivered to the county authorities in Lumberton. "We make a request," it read, "that our wives who were arrested a few days ago and placed in jail be released to come home to their families by Monday morning. . . . If not, the Bloodiest times will be here that ever was before—the life of every man will be in jeopardy."

Though the authorities were initially unmoved, the fearful reaction of the rest of the white populace of Robeson County forced them to capitulate, and the women were released. By the summer of 1871, as the violence continued—the release of the wives was followed shortly thereafter by the assassination of a Police Guard captain who had participated in the murders of Allen and William Lowrie—U.S. troops had been called in to the county. Their commander, John Gorman, who was the North Carolina adjutant general, arranged to meet with Henry Berry Lowrie to see if he would be willing to surrender. By this point, many of the white citizens of the county had become convinced of the futility of capturing or destroying the gang and were willing to allow Lowrie and his followers to

The Robeson County courthouse, in the yard of which Henderson Oxendine, a member of the Lowrie Gang, was hanged on March 17, 1871. Oxendine was the only member of the gang to be legally executed.

leave the county unharmed if they pledged never to return.

According to Gorman, his two-hour meeting with the Robin Hood of the Lumbees was cordial. The members of the gang, observed Strong, all wore homespun clothing, were "formidably armed," and were in "the prime of young manhood and . . . the best of health." Henry Berry Lowrie himself was armed with a "Spencer rifle, a double-barreled shotgun, two revolvers, and a bowie knife; each of his men carried a double-barreled shotgun apiece and several revolvers." After thanking

the official for coming, Lowrie tried to justify his crimes and proclaimed his innocence of many of the killings attributed to him. To Gorman, the outlaw seemed tired of his life on the run, and he asked if, upon their surrender, he and his men would be permitted to "harmlessly go" to a "remote part of the public domain," as other Indians who had come into conflict with whites had been allowed to do.

Gorman responded that he did not have the authority to approve such an arrangement, then asked Lowrie why, if they were weary, he and his men did not simply disappear from the county. "Robeson County is the only land I know," the outlaw replied. "I can hardly read, and do not know where to go if I leave these woods and swamps, where I was raised. If I can get safe conduct and pardon I will go anywhere. . . . But these people will not let me live and I do not mean to enter any jail again." Though Gorman met with Lowrie several more times, he was un-able to convince the state government to agree to the outlaws' terms for surrender. Instead, the legislature increased the reward money offered for the gang's capture, to which Lowrie responded by leading a morning raid on Lumberton itself. The gang hauled the safes from the town's biggest store and the sheriff's offices—Lumberton had no bank—emptied them of their contents of $22,000, and tauntingly aban-

The February 16, 1872, raid on Lumberton was the last great exploit of the Lowrie gang. The outlaws entered the town at dawn and hauled away iron safes from a department store and the sheriff's office on a cart; when the safes proved too heavy, they dumped them on an avenue and made off with their contents.

doned them in the middle of Main Street.

But the great Lumberton caper was destined to be the last hurrah for the Lowrie Gang. Soon afterward, Henry Berry Lowrie disappeared from public view, never to be seen again; over the next two years the remainder of his gang was hunted down and killed by lawmen or bounty hunters.

Henry Berry Lowrie's fate remains a mystery. Many Lumbee prefer to believe that he remained elusive to the end and escaped Robeson County. Various stories are told explaining how this happened, of his subsequent life in the West and his supposed return visits to attend funerals or weddings or other family gatherings. Many years later, his nephew, the Reverend D. F. Lowry, maintained that Henry Berry had left Robeson County in early 1872 with the aid of John Gorman, who outfitted the fugitive in a soldier's uniform, had his face wrapped in bandages to disguise his identity, and shipped him off aboard a train filled with wounded soldiers. D. F. Lowry's son, Dr. Earl Lowry, maintains that the outlaw leader used an elaborate scheme involving a rabbit carcass, a straw dummy, and a phony coffin to fake his own death and then, wearing a soldier's uniform, left the county on a northbound train. According to this version, the scourge of Robeson County then went on to serve four years in the army before being dis-

charged in Virginia. Another story tells of a live Lowrie leaving Robeson County on a train in a specially designed coffin, drilled with airholes and presumably marked to be delivered for burial at some far destination.

Several scenarios are also given for how Lowrie met his death. Though they vary in their particulars, the most common and plausible maintain that he accidentally shot himself with his own gun soon after the great Lumberton raid, and that his cohorts, determined that his corpse should be neither dishonored nor claimed by a bounty hunter, buried him in a secret location near the Devil's Den. If Rhoda, Lowrie's widow, knew what happened to her husband, she never said. (She lived for many more years after his disappearance.) But to most Lumbee, an irrefutable explanation for the mystery of Lowrie's disappearance is irrelevant. "It doesn't matter how he died, or when he died, or where his body lies for its dust," said one Lumbee, expressing a common point of view. "It's his spirit that counts." The outlaw condemned by white society is the most enduring hero of the Lumbee people, who celebrate his courage, his strength as a leader, his resourcefulness, his opposition to injustice, and his willingness to fight for his people. He remains an inspiration to the Lumbee in their battle against the racial hatred and discrimination that they continue to encounter all too often in their daily lives.

Anderson Locklear and some of his students at the Croatan Normal School around 1910. The following year, the school changed its name to the Indian Normal School of Robeson County.

MIND
AND
SPIRIT

Though the end of the Lowrie War restored peace to Robeson County, the Lumbee's struggle for respect and equality was still far from over.

Perhaps the greatest obstacle the Lumbee faced as far as improving their social and economic standing was education. Near the end of *Reconstruction*, as the approximately 12-year-period of economic, political, and social readjustment in the South following the Civil War was known, the government of North Carolina provided for the establishment of a segregated public school system, meaning that separate public schools would be established for whites and for blacks. (Previously, the state had made little, if any, provision for the public education of its young citizens of any color.) However, no specific provisions were made for Indians, who, it was assumed, as legally classified "people of color" would attend black schools. (After 1835, Lumbee children had generally not attended school. Prior to 1835, a few Lumbees had attended school with whites.)

The Lumbee regarded being made to attend black schools as a tacit denial of their special identity and heritage as well as a continuation of the discrimination to which they had been subjected since the enactment of the Free Negro Codes in 1835. Most Lumbee refused to attend the black schools. Their reluctance was less a matter of adopting the racist assumptions of their white neighbors than an insistence on their own unique identity and equal social status. The Lumbee objected to attending black schools not so much out of any prejudice against blacks but because to do so was to acquiesce in white-imposed definitions of their own supposed inferiority.

From 1875 to 1885, a period of time remembered by the Lumbee as the Decade of Despair, the Indians of Robeson

County opposed their state's government by insisting on their right to schools of their own. Finally, their arguments were given a sympathetic listen by Hamilton McMillan, a state representative from the county. After studying the origins of the Lumbee, McMillan became convinced that the Indians were, as they had always claimed, the descendants of the Roanoke colonists and the coastal Indians that some sources had referred to as the Croatan.

The representative then brought before the North Carolina General Assembly a proposed piece of legislation with two provisions. One would officially name the Lumbee the "Croatan Indians of Robeson County." With this new designation, the Lumbee would at last receive legal recognition of their Indianness. The legislation's second provision stated "that the said Indians and their descendants shall have separate schools for their children, school committees of their own race and color and shall be allowed to select teachers of their own choice."

The act was passed in 1885, but it had little immediate effect on Lumbee students. Although the Lumbee were now permitted to create their own schools, they were not given the funding needed to establish quality educational facilities. Even more frustrating was the lack of potential instructors among the Lumbee. Because very few Robeson County Indians had attended school in the past 50 years, virtually none of them were qualified to teach.

The Reverend W. L. Moore, a Methodist minister, was the first principal of the Lumbee Normal School. Moore was the individual most responsible for securing separate public education for the Indians of Robeson County.

McMillan again brought the Lumbee's difficulties to the attention of the General Assembly by sponsoring a bill that provided for the establishment of an Indian normal school (a school designed for the training of teachers) in Robeson County. The bill, which was signed into law in 1887, also appropriated $500 to pay the school's instructors. However, no allocation was made for the construction of the facility. If the Lumbee were to have their school, they would have to build it themselves.

At first, the Lumbee were wary of the enterprise. Years of discrimination had taught them to be distrustful of the state government, so most found it difficult to lend their support to any school that received state funds. Slowly, the seven Lumbee men who had been named to the school's board of trustees, especially a respected Methodist minister named W. L. Moore, convinced their people to abandon their suspicions. After donating $1,000 in materials and labor, the Lumbee proudly witnessed the opening of the Croatan Normal School in 1887. Moore, who had been trained at another normal school, was selected as the school's first principal. The first class consisted of 15 students.

In 1889, the legislature increased its annual appropriation to the Croatan Normal School to $1,000, but it was soon clear that the school would need much more money than that if it were to combat illiteracy and the other educational deficiencies caused by the state's long neglect of the Lumbee community. The next year, Moore re-

This one-room schoolhouse, known as the Oxendine School, was typical of many of the educational facilities the Lumbee established for their children after 1885.

Preston Locklear was one of seven members of the first board of trustees for the Indian Normal School. Like many Lumbees, Locklear derived some of his livelihood from the forests of Robeson County, and he met his death while gathering turpentine from the pines.

quested additional funds from the *Bureau of Indian Affairs (BIA)*, the department of the federal government responsible for dealing with Indian groups. In a letter to the BIA, the principal emphasized the great educational progress already made by Lumbee children, explaining that "the youth who have had (to some degree) better opportunities for educating themselves show that the moral, intellectual, and social aptitudes in them are real."

The BIA's response was disappointing. The agency's commissioner wrote that it could not afford to help finance the school. The federal government, he explained, was already responsible for the education of about 36,000 Indian children and had sufficient funds to serve only half of them. The commissioner regarded the Lumbee as a "civilized tribe," and as such he believed them to be better equipped to find their own means of funding the school than Indians less assimilated into the American mainstream. Though it was not enough to earn them equal treatment under the law in Robeson County, their ancestors' early adoption of the ways and values of non-Indians were now being used to penalize the Lumbee in their dealings with the federal government.

Without federal and additional state funding, the Croatan Normal School faced continual financial hardship, but

This building served as the Indian Normal School from 1887 to 1909, when a new, larger structure was built nearer Pembroke.

When this photograph was taken around 1923, the building that would become known as Old Main (center) was the newest incarnation of the Indian Normal School, which was then officially known as the Cherokee Indian Normal School of Robeson County.

the Lumbee's commitment to education somehow enabled the institution to continue operating. In 1905, the Reverend D. F. Lowry received the first diploma issued by the school for completing its "scientific course." Years later, Lowry recalled that the curriculum had been far from standardized. Instead of following a set program in their classwork, the school's students were encouraged to pursue "anything they could handle."

The school's success inspired the legislature to allocate $3,000 to build a larger facility in 1909. At the new building on the outskirts of Pembroke, the number of students increased, and the quality of instruction improved. The school also soon acquired a new name, as did the tribe. Some local whites had taken to shortening the name Croatan Indians to Cro. Probably because it sounded like "Jim Crow," an informal name for the southern laws that imposed segregation and other injustices, the Lumbee considered "Cro" to be a racial slur. The state legislature agreed to drop the word Croatan from the Lumbee's official name in 1911. Thus, they became known as the Indians of Robeson County and the school was re-christened the Indian Normal School of Robeson County.

The name change did not entirely please the Lumbee. Many felt the designation was too ambiguous. Still struggling to be recognized by all as an Indian people, these Lumbee wanted a name that clearly defined them as culturally and socially distinct from their non-Indian neighbors.

In 1913, the legislature came up with yet another name for the Lumbee: the Cherokee Indians of Robeson County. The name resulted from the contention of several scholars that in the early 18th century some Cherokee had integrated with the Lumbee. According to this theory, Cherokee warriors joined the forces of Colonel John Barnwell, who had been sent by the colonial government of South Carolina to battle the Tuscarora Indians of North Carolina, who, angered by the loss of their lands to whites, had risen up against the settlers in 1711.

Barnwell was unable to put down the uprising and signed a truce with the Tuscarora. (The Indian rebels were defeated two years later by another force of troops.) On his way back to South Carolina, Barnwell and his men are said to have marched through Robeson County. Lumbee tradition holds that some Cherokee warriors decided to stay there and that they merged with the Lumbee people.

The name of the Lumbee's school was likewise changed to the Cherokee Indian Normal School. Under this appellation, the institution saw its greatest expansion. Over the next two decades, the leadership of such educators as Judge L. R. Varser, professors T. C. Henderson, A. B. Riley, and S. B. Smithy, and the Reverend Oscar R. Sampson helped the school grow and prosper. The 1920s also saw the establishment of several new elementary and secondary schools for Lumbee children. This network of community schools would eventually help make the Lumbee the best-educated Indian people in the country.

The Lumbee's commitment to education enabled their schools to survive one of the greatest threats ever to their existence—the *Great Depression*. Following the stock market crash of 1929, the United States was plunged into the greatest economic crisis of its history, as businesses and banks failed, unemployment skyrocketed, and millions of Americans lost their jobs and their homes. Like most educational institutions, the Lumbee's schools suddenly faced a dire financial crisis greater than any they had previously known. But whereas many schools were forced to cut back on their operations during these hardest of times, the Cherokee Indian Normal School, under the leadership of J. E. Sawyer and G. C. Maughon, was still able to expand and

For the Lumbee, the Christian religion has been almost as significant a unifying force as education. The Lumbee belong to a variety of different Protestant denominations. Here, the congregation of the Prospect United Methodist Church, the nation's largest Indian church, is gathered for the church's centennial celebration in 1974.

added a college curriculum. In 1940, the North Carolina legislature recognized the school's significance as an institution of higher learning by changing its name to Pembroke State College for Indians; that year the first four-year college degrees were given to five members of the graduating class. At the time, Pembroke was the only state-supported four-year college for Indians in the United States.

The hard work and dedication that led to the founding of Pembroke helped to unite the Lumbee throughout the late 19th and early 20th centuries. Perhaps equally important in bringing the Lumbee people together were the religious institutions they supported.

No one knows exactly when the Lumbee were first exposed to Christianity. If Lumbee oral tradition is accurate, their knowledge of Christian religion dates from the time the Hatteras Indians merged with the Roanoke colonists in the late 16th century. Historical sources make clear that by the early 18th century, Christianity was the major religious influence in Lumbee religious life. At this time, the Lumbee had no churches. They either worshiped with other family members in homes or at outdoor gatherings.

By the early 19th century, a few Lumbees were attending formal services in white churches. In order to maintain control over their own religious lives, the Lumbee eventually built their own houses of worship, most of which were associated with Baptist and Methodist sects. According to oral tradition, the earliest of these churches were named New Hope, Thessalonica, Union Chapel, Old Dogwood, Reedy Branch, Burnt Swamp, Old Prospect, New Jerusalem, and Saint Annah.

In 1880, a group of Lumbee Baptists created the tribe's first formal religious organization. The group's first meeting was moderated by Carl Wilkins, a Lumbee, and held at the Burnt Swamp Church. The new organization took the name *Burnt Swamp Association of the Mixed Race.* (Like most other Lumbee institutions, the association's name changed over time. It became known as the Burnt Swamp Association of the Croatan Race in 1885. Later, "Croatan" was dropped from the name.)

In the late 19th century, Lumbee Methodists became factionalized into two groups. About half felt that the Lumbee needed more control over the local Methodist organization. In 1900, under the leadership of Henry H. Lowry, they established the Holiness Methodist Church of Lumbee River Annual Conference (also known as the Lumbee Methodist Conference). The other Lumbee Methodists were content to continue their affiliation with the white-run Methodist Episcopal Church. Among their ranks was W. L. Moore, who helped establish 10 Indian churches in the North Carolina Conference of the United Methodist Church.

Despite the Lumbee's devotion to Christianity, they retained some beliefs that predated their contact with whites. Like all Indian peoples of North and South America, the Lumbee once practiced their own native religion. But unlike many Indian groups, by the early 20th century the tribe had no knowledge of the rituals and ceremonies performed by their ancestors. The Lumbee had taken on European ways so completely, so long ago, that the formal rites of their original religion had been forgotten. Only in their oral tradition did any remnant of their old religion survive.

Recounted in these stories are certain beliefs about the supernatural. On the surface, most of these ideas seem to contradict Christian doctrine. Nevertheless, most Christian Lumbee, in the past and in the present, have had little trouble accepting both what they have learned in church and what they have been taught by their elders throughout their lives.

This merging of Christian and traditional beliefs is perhaps best seen in the career of Reverend Moore. Both in his role as a supporter of the Croatan Normal School and the Methodist Episcopal Church, Moore revealed his sympathy with the views of most local non-Indian leaders. Like them, he regarded non-Indian-style education and Christianity as essential to the advancement of the Lumbee people.

Yet at the same time, Moore retained his ancestors' belief that there existed a spirit realm that frequently interacted with the physical world of humans. The minister's descendants still tell stories of Moore's talent for predicting a death in the Lumbee community. Moore and his family often heard loud noises in their house, which the reverend maintained were messages from beyond. As he explained to his children, the sounds were the spirits' way of letting him know that he would soon have to preach at a funeral. Such noisy visitations from spirits—called *totens*, or *tokens*—were considered almost commonplace in the Lumbee community.

Some Lumbees also claimed to receive warnings of the imminent death of a loved one in dreams. Others found a similar meaning in certain actions of birds. As in certain other eastern Indian cultures, a bird flying into a Lumbee family's home was considered a sign that a member of the family would soon die. It was believed that the bird had come to retrieve the doomed person's spirit. The Lumbee believed that the only way to ensure the family's safety was to capture the bird and release it unharmed after requesting that the animal allow the spirit to stay with its family a while longer. Similarly, a rooster coming on the porch to crow was believed to herald an imminent death.

Another common Lumbee belief shared by other Native Americans was an association between snakes and rain. Whenever their fields were dry, Lumbee farmers killed a snake and hung it on a tree limb. This ritual was thought to bring rain.

Individual Lumbees known as *cup readers* were believed to be able to locate anything from lost keys to lost people by examining the signs left in the bottom of a coffee cup. One of the most dramatic instances of a cup reader's talents involves the disappearance of Marcus Dial in 1932. When it was discovered that the 94-year-old Dial was missing, one of his sons tried to find his father's footprints, but rain had washed away any trace of where the elderly man had wandered. After leading a communitywide search for several days, Dial's family decided to consult a cup reader named Nepsie Brayboy. After examining the cup, she told them, "Marcus was looking for his son's house and strayed off into the woods near this house." Following her instructions, the family found Dial's body the next day. Several family members later claimed that the tragedy might have been averted if the cup reader had been consulted earlier.

Another special power valued by the Lumbee was the ability to *blow fire*, which was thought to be a gift from God bestowed only on people whose father had died while they were in the womb. The power to blow fire allowed a person to relieve the pain and blistering of burn victims by gently massaging and blowing on the injured area. This practice, along with the use of medicinal plants and herbs, enabled the Lumbee to take care of their own before the advent of hospitals and burn centers.

The people with the greatest mystical gifts were known as *conjurers*. Authentic conjurers were said to have sold their souls to the devil in exchange for particularly extraordinary powers, such as the ability to predict the future and perform various types of magical feats.

Many stories are told about a conjurer named Aaron Carter. According to one tale, Carter had a bitter enemy who swore to kill him. The man never succeeded, however, because whenever he pointed a gun at Carter he was mysteriously unable to pull the trigger. Many Lumbees also claimed to have offered Carter a ride after spotting him walking along a road. Carter always declined. To the drivers' surprise, when they reached their destination Carter would be there to meet them. Other conjurers were said to be able to predict the future or influence other people's actions merely by their presence. Accused criminals sometimes brought conjurers to their trials in the hope that their powerful presence might help sway the jury.

Much Lumbee folk belief concerned death and funeral customs. The bed of a seriously ill person would always be moved so that it faced the east, and those who visited the person after his bed had been turned would immediately know that he or she was expected to die. If the patient did fail to recover, his or her corpse was placed on a "cooling board" until a pine coffin was ready. Some Lumbee men made their coffins years in advance and stored them in their barns, a custom that is still practiced by some Lumbees. After the coffin was built, the "setting up" began; it usually lasted for two days, during which the deceased's friends and family came by to pay their respects and "set up" with the corpse. The setting up was an opportunity for the community to

The original Harpers Ferry Baptist Church in Robeson County. The Baptists are the largest denomination among the Lumbee.

demonstrate its support and sympathy for the family of the deceased; it served also as a social outlet and a reaffirmation of social values. Young people often used the setting up to meet members of the opposite sex, while the adults generally sat around the fireplace talking and reminiscing. Before the corpse was actually taken inside a church for the funeral service, a Lumbee elder would "line out" (demonstrate by singing) an appropriate hymn for the congregation to sing, a practice made necessary by the low literacy rate and general lack of hymnbooks among the Lumbee. Although the necessity for it has lessened, the tradition of lining out hymns still survives in some Lumbee congregations.

In the difficult years following the Civil War until the mid-20th century, schools and churches—the institutions that fed the mind and the spirit of Lumbee individuals—also helped shape the Lumbee community. Like their non-Indian neighbors, the Lumbee valued education, but having their own school system gave the tribe even more than an educated populace. Their school system provided the Lumbee with a source of pride and a means of distinguishing themselves from the whites and blacks with whom they shared the region. Though, like their non-Indian neighbors, the Lumbee were Christians, they wanted to practice their religion in their own way—a need that moved them to form their own churches and religious organizations while combining their folk beliefs with Christian doctrine to create a worldview that was uniquely Lumbee. ▲

A Lumbee girl picks cotton. Among the Lumbee, every member of the family participated in picking cotton; some Lumbee children could pick as much as 100 pounds of cotton in a single day.

A LIVING
FROM THE
LAND

Before the arrival of non-Indians, most eastern Indians were farmers. The Lumbee were no exception, but they abandoned their native agricultural techniques long before other Indian groups in the region did so. It took much longer, however, for the Lumbee to change their *reason* for tilling the soil. When Europeans first began to come to Robeson County in large numbers, the Lumbee usually grew only enough food to feed themselves, but from the settlers they learned instead to plant cash crops. A Lumbee family could sell cash crops at a market and then spend the profits to buy the food that they used to produce themselves.

A typical Lumbee farmer in the last decades of the 19th century and first decades of the 20th century cultivated about 40 acres and planted about half of this land with cash crops, such as cotton and tobacco. (Today, Lumbee farmers are far more likely to devote the majority of their acreage to small grain and tobacco.) On most of the remaining land, they grew corn, garden vegetables (such as tomatoes, cabbage, peas, okra, collards, turnips, and beans), and potatoes. The garden vegetables and the potatoes were eaten by the farmer's family; the corn was used to feed both the family and its livestock. A small plot was also planted with hay, wheat, and oats as fodder for farm animals.

Most Lumbee farmers raised chickens and hogs. Although both of these animals were introduced to North America by Europeans, they became such a part of Lumbee life that some of the oldest tribe members today contend that they were always in the Lumbee homeland. In the course of his travels through North Carolina in the first decade of the 18th century, John Lawson reported being given two chickens by Indians along the coast; since such fowl were not native to the continent, he re-

Lumbee children help an older family member prepare tobacco leaves for curing. By the last decade of the 19th century, tobacco had replaced cotton as the most important cash crop for Lumbee farmers.

garded the gift as a sure sign of previous contact with white settlers.

An average Lumbee farmer kept 50 to 60 hens, in order to ensure a steady supply of eggs, and at least 1 rooster for every 20 hens, in order to ensure the continuance of the stock. Like other farmers of the era, the Lumbee relied on roosters as a timepiece. The sound of their crowing signaled daybreak and the start of the farmer's working day.

A chicken dinner was a special treat, usually reserved for an evening when the local preacher came to visit. On these occasions, one of the family's children would have the responsibility of chasing down the chicken to be served.

The slaughtering of hogs was a much more social event. *Slaughter Day* was a time for families and neighbors to come together both to work at a difficult task and to enjoy each other's friendship.

People never came to a hog killing empty-handed. Everyone brought knives, tables, and pots. By two o'clock

continued on page 81

NEW TRADITIONS

In light of the ability of his people to draw strength from their traditional identity as Native Americans while assimilating other, more modern cultural values, it is not surprising to find a Lumbee artist, Lloyd Oxendine, as curator of the American Indian Community House Gallery-Museum in New York City, an institution dedicated to the promotion of contemporary Indian art. In 1969, Oxendine, who is now 50 years old and was born and raised in Pembroke, North Carolina, founded (also in New York City) the very first gallery of contemporary Indian art in the country.

Although he acknowledges the importance of traditional Indian handiwork and artifacts as objets d'art—"I realize now that everything is based on tradition," he says—at his gallery Oxendine emphasizes the work of the many talented Native American artists who are working in a more modern vein. "Previously, the idea of Indians doing contemporary art wasn't acceptable; it was only acceptable as

arts and crafts," he points out. "So what I've accomplished, and am still accomplishing, is making Native American art marketable and acceptable."

Just as the Lumbee draw on their past to prepare for the future, Oxendine's art encompasses both the traditional and the modern. His work with acrylics and other materials, seen in this section, is quintessentially modern, yet it is resonant with themes and ideas of longstanding importance to all American Indian peoples. In doing so, it takes a place among the many new traditions being forged daily by the Lumbee.

Prophecy; *acrylic on canvas, 1991.*

Prairie Grass, Barbed Wire; *acrylic on canvas, 1988.*

Seven Birches; *acrylic on canvas, 1987.*

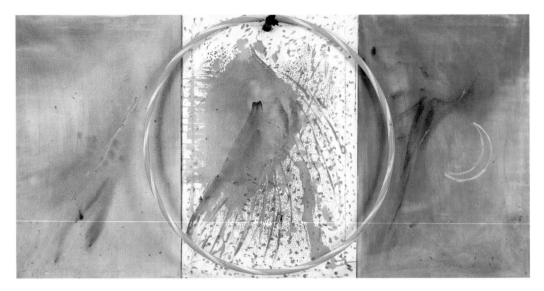

Sacred Hoop; *mixed media, 1991.*

Lodgepole Pines; *acrylic on canvas, 1987.*

Rape of Canyon de Chelly; *acrylic on canvas, 1989.*

Didn't Want To Go to War; *mixed media, 1992.*

Don't Ask Why; *mixed media, 1991.*

Warrior Shield; *mixed media, 1991.*

80

continued from page 72

in the morning, long before the rooster crowed, they were already building huge fires over which they would boil pots of water. In the absence of a thermometer, the temperature of the water was tested by hand. At the proper temperature—150 to 155 degrees—a person could stick in his hand twice quickly in succession, but the third time would be unbearable.

Once the water was right, the men set about killing the hogs, an exciting enterprise for a people dependent on pork for much of their diet. According to one Lumbee elder, "Ten or twelve hogs weighing about three hundred pounds each and waiting for the knife was a beautiful sight." The Lumbee men were also responsible for dressing (cutting up) the carcasses. Once this task was completed, the women began their work by scraping the animals' intestines clean so that they could later be used as sausage casings.

Everyone then took a break for dinner. Dinner was perhaps the most anticipated part of slaughter day, providing the host family with a chance to show their appreciation of the labor and skill volunteered by relatives and friends. The meal usually consisted of collards, corn bread, baked sweet po-

The Lumbees (from left) Olen Woods, Fuller Lloyd, Henry Lowry, Carlen Clark, Elais Harris, and Burney Hunt at a hog killing in 1952. Hog killings are an important communal activity in the Lumbee community.

tatoes, boiled backbone, fried lean tenderloins, and hot black coffee, all of it plentiful.

As soon as dinner was over, the workers, well fed and well rested, completed the chore of processing the hog meat. First, the lean meat was stuffed into the sausage casings. Then, the livers were boiled, ground, and mixed with onions, sage, and cracklings to make a pudding. (Cracklings, or fried pork skins, were also a favorite wintertime treat.) Sometimes blood was added to the ground liver as a flavoring. The resulting dish was called blood pudding.

The fat trimmed from the meat was placed in wash pots and cooked into lard. This slow process required careful supervision because the lard in an unwatched pot could easily become scorched. While cooking, the lard was stirred with a green sweet bay stick that had been cut from the local woods. When it was nearly done, bay leaves were put into the pot to give the lard an appealing aroma.

At the same time, other laborers prepared the hams, shoulders, and middlings. Before the Civil War, the Lumbee smoked their meat, but in the late 19th century, they began using salt to preserve pork. Once cured, the meat was washed with warm water. After a brief drying period, it was rubbed with a combination of borax and homegrown red pepper. Stored in a smokehouse, the meat was then ready to be eaten throughout the year. Until the mid-20th century, the pork processed on Slaughter Day was one of the staples of a Lumbee family's diet. Although the Lumbee are now much less dependent on this food source, hog killings remain an important part of Lumbee culture.

"Woodsawing" was another activity that brought the Lumbee community together for hard work and socializing. The family hosting a woodsawing would fell a number of trees during the day, then invite relatives and friends to spend three or four hours that night cutting the logs into pieces small enough to fit into a stove or fireplace. The goal of a woodsawing was to provide the hosts with enough firewood to last a year.

While the men sawed, the women prepared a huge feast that was enjoyed by all once the work was done. After the meal, the diners drank coffee or a few drams of whiskey and talked about the year's crops, their latest hunting trips, or any of the many other aspects of Lumbee life. After World War II, with the development of chain saws and other technology that makes it possible for an individual to lay in his own store of wood, the importance of woodsawing as a communal event among the Lumbee began to decline. Undoubtedly the machines are quicker, but the Lumbee community has lost an important expression of cooperation, community, and solidarity.

House and barn raisings were other tasks that demanded community cooperation. Building a house or barn required moving logs that were far too heavy for a single person or even a fam-

Lumbees pose for a photograph at a communal gathering at the home of Dougal Brooks in 1950. Such gatherings, often centered on the performance of a task essential to a family's well-being, such as woodcutting, cornshucking, or quilting, served both the social and economic needs of the Lumbee community.

ily to lift alone. At a raising, a team of laborers stacked logs on top of one another to create a structure's walls. (The roof was later added by the owner and covered with wooden shingles.)

Another major chore that was performed communally was logrolling— clearing farmland by cutting down all the trees that stood on it and rolling the logs into a huge pile for burning. In the heavily forested Lumbee homeland, full-grown trees sometimes grew more than 100 feet tall. The trunks and limbs of the tallest trees could be moved only through the combined efforts of many

strong and determined men. After the trees had been removed, the men, women, and children all joined together to clear the field of roots, stumps, and other debris. As with so many other community events, a logrolling ended with a huge meal.

Although families usually tended their own fields, responsibility for certain farming chores was shared by other members of the community. For instance, after the corn harvest, a family often invited neighbors over to help shuck the crop. At every corn shucking, a jug of jimmy-john (homemade whis-

Although its importance to the community as a whole has declined since the 19th century, some Lumbees still earn money by extracting turpentine from Robeson County's pine forests. Seen here are black turpentine gatherers at work in nearby Sampson County.

key) was placed in the center of a large pile of corn. It was understood that no one would be allowed a sip until all the corn had been shucked. Any man who found a red ear in the pile was rewarded with a kiss from the woman of his choice.

A far less pleasant chore was pulling fodder. This difficult job, which involved pulling the blades from cornstalks, had to be done in August, the hottest month in the oppressive southern summer. After being removed, the dried blades were then tied together to create bundles of fodder. Feeding fodder to horses and mules cut down a Lumbee farmer's expenses because it allowed him to avoid devoting precious acres of farmland to raising other animal foods, such as hay and oats.

Most chores were performed by all members of a farming family. But a few jobs were only done by women or only done by men. For instance, women were responsible for making quilts. Several well-made quilts were essential possessions for each Lumbee family. Late on winter nights, after the blaze in the fireplace had died down, the Lumbee relied on quilts to keep them warm. A Lumbee elder recently recalled the chill of the early morning in the era before central heating:

The minute your feet touched that cold floor you came awake. Rambling around in the dark house looking for matches to start a fire in the fireplace and kitchen stove, the lazy man returned to his bed until the house got warmer, while the energetic one crawled into his clothes and went to the barn to begin his chores.

Quilts were made at quilting parties. Months in advance, a party's hostess began cutting squares of fabric from old clothes and empty flour sacks in her free time. Her children helped out by picking the seeds out of cotton from the family's fields. This cotton would be used as padding inside the quilt. Some evenings, children were told that they could not go to bed until they had filled their shoes with cotton seeds.

The serious work began on the day of the quilting party. The hostess and her friends first stitched all the fabric squares together into one multicolored piece to create the quilt's top. The top was then sewn to the quilt bottom, with the cotton filler in between. As a quilter had to have both great patience and extraordinary sewing skill, the ability to make a good quilt was a source of pride among Lumbee women. One Lumbee woman once boasted that she had achieved her life's ambition the day she had completed her 100th quilt.

Some Lumbee gatherings were unrelated to work. Church services provided a chance for Christian Lumbees to socialize. Events revolving around their schools—a justifiable source of pride for the Lumbee community—were also invariably well attended. The most popular of these was *School Breaking*, a celebration that marked the end of the school year and the beginning of summer. As the end of the school year coincided with the time by which every diligent farmer should have his acres plowed, his year's crop in, and his fields well attended in anticipation of the harvest that was still several months distant, virtually every member of the Lumbee community, as well as the students themselves, were free to participate. Even those Lumbee engaged in a trade or profession usually took a holiday, for the community would have little need of their services on School-Breaking Day.

The morning of School-Breaking Day, women prepared huge amounts of food, enough for their family and often a few dozen of their friends. Men plowed their fields and gave their livestock enough grain and fodder to last them until sundown. School Breaking was an all-day event, so everyone made sure to finish their daily chores before the festivities began.

Families and friends gathered on the school grounds early in the day. By noon, a long table was already groaning under the weight of all the food made for the occasion, but before anyone could touch the glorious spread, the principal had to deliver his blessing— always a cause for good-natured grumbling. As one Lumbee put it, "Sometimes the blessing was too long for a good appetite."

In addition to the food brought by the celebrants, refreshments were sold at School Breaking. Hot dog and ice cream concessions were common, but lemonade was the Lumbee's favorite treat. Local peddlers also came to the

A turpentine distillery in Sampson County. With the decline of Robeson County's pine forests in the last decades of the 19th century, many Lumbees left their homeland to work in the turpentine industry in Georgia. Such economically motivated migration would become even more prevalent in the 20th century.

grounds, certain of finding many customers among the crowd. There was often music and dancing, and it was not unusual to see an individual or a small group of Lumbees sneaking off to the woods for a drink of "stumphole"— home-brewed hard liquor. The revelry invariably lasted until well after nightfall, but the next morning, all too early, the daily routine of work began anew.

Not every Lumbee worked a farm, of course. Some preferred to work for wages, and many had jobs in the lumber industry. One popular job among Lumbee men was transporting lumber to market. Trees felled by lumberjacks were rolled into the Lumber River, where Lumbee workers would collect the heavy logs and tie them together to create a raft, which they would then ride down the Lumber to the Pee Dee River and on to Georgetown, South Carolina, where the lumber could be sold.

The ride was difficult. The workers had to be constantly on the lookout for shoals and snags, which they had to navigate carefully to avoid grounding the raft, all the while fighting off swarms of mosquitoes and other insects—some of whose bites bred disease—and avoiding the ever-present water moccasins in the swamplands. Still, many men loved the trip downriver, which provided them with a chance to hunt, fish, and swap tales with their friends, free of the constraints of a time clock or the rising and setting of the sun. If the river was relatively free of obstructions and the water was high, the trip to Georgetown took about three weeks; the journey home—a distance of more than 100 miles—was made on foot.

A trip similar in kind was made by some Lumbees from Pembroke to Fayetteville, North Carolina—a distance of about 40 miles—to bring turkeys to market. The trip usually took several days and was made by foot, with the turkeys being driven along by the walkers. At night, the turkey herders made an open-air camp; as they cooked their meal and slept, the gobblers roosted in the surrounding trees. In the morning, the Lumbees rounded up their flock and continued on their way.

A small number of Lumbees found jobs in the turpentine industry. The rich pine forests in Robeson County had made the gathering of turpentine profitable prior to the Civil War, but after Sherman's troops burned many of the forests to the ground, the industry fell into decline, and fewer and fewer Lumbee could make a living tapping the pines. In the 1880s, some workers left their homes for Georgia, where the turpentine industry was still thriving. For most, the move proved painful; they missed not only their families but also the unique Lumbee way of life that they knew could not be duplicated in a new state or anywhere outside of Robeson County. A few decided to remain in Georgia, but by the early 20th century most had returned. The Lumbee's attachment to Robeson County would, as the 20th century progressed and technological and social developments diminished the importance of such communal gatherings as Slaughter Day and woodsawings, ensure not only that the Lumbee would survive as a distinct Indian people but that their struggle for recognition and equality in their homeland would continue. ▲

A Lumbee couple, Elisha Locklear and Lillie Jane Brooks, in 1925.

MAKING
THE
FUTURE

Aside from the establishment of their educational system, perhaps the most noteworthy event affecting the Lumbee in the late 19th and early 20th centuries was the founding of the city of Pembroke, which today is one of the largest towns in Robeson County and the most important settlement in which the Lumbee predominate—they make up nearly 90 percent of Pembroke's population. The community began to develop in the 1890s around the intersection of the two railroad lines—one running north-south, one running east-west—that bisected Robeson County. The very name Pembroke reflects the importance of the railroad to the town in its early days; Pembroke was probably named after Pembroke Jones, an official with the Wilmington and Weldon Railroad.

Initially the town consisted of a small number of wooden buildings that fronted on dirt sidewalks and unpaved roads. Most of the businesses served the needs of the many farmers in the surrounding countryside in one way or another. The most important of these, since the 1920s (the decade in which the first brick building in Pembroke was constructed), has been Pates Supply Company, a general store that supplies feed, implements, fertilizers, and all the other equipment and provisions needed by the modern farmer. Today, Pembroke looks much like other small towns in rural areas around the country. It has also been, since 1909, the home of the institution that began as the Croatan Normal School and is now Pembroke State University.

Pembroke's political history in some ways mirrors the larger struggle of the Lumbee in the 20th century for equality and a greater control of their own destiny. The terms of the town's incorporation in 1895 provided for the election of the municipal government—a mayor and four commissioners—by the town's residents. Though whites were, even then, a minority in Pembroke, they were able to maintain control of the city government by using various machinations to keep the Lumbee from voting. By 1917, however, the Lumbee majority in Pembroke was so overwhelming that they were virtually assured of political control, whereupon the white citizens of the town succeeded in persuading the state legislature to change the method whereby city officials were selected. The mayor and commissioners were now to be selected by the governor, assuring the continuation of white political power in Pembroke. Finally, in 1947, at the insistence of the Lumbee, democratic elections were restored; all of the town's mayors since then have been Lumbees, and often—as at the present time—the entire town government has been manned by Lumbees.

The 1940s were in general a time of great change for the Lumbee. Many of them served in the armed forces of the United States during World War II, and over 40 were killed. (Several decades earlier, many Lumbees had also volunteered for service in World War I; 13 were killed in the fighting in France, and the company in which they served earned a reputation for conspicuous bravery.) Before serving in the military, few of these Lumbee soldiers had ventured far from Robeson County; the two

A Lumbee gathering in Harpers Ferry, Robeson County, in 1945. At the time the Indians of Robeson County were still officially known as the Cherokee Indians of Robeson County.

Following World War II and the Korean War, black servicemen returned to their homes in the South to find that under segregation they were still second-class citizens. Returned Lumbee veterans in Robeson County had similar experiences.

world wars thus provided many Lumbees with their first opportunity for extensive contact with the outside world. Particularly after World War II, many Lumbee veterans returned to Robeson County with a different perspective on the social issues affecting their homeland. Having risked their lives for their country, they were less willing to accept the prejudice and discrimination that was a part of everyday life in Robeson County, where all public facilities and accomodations, except in Pembroke, were segregated according to race—white, Indian, or black. The experience of one returned Lumbee serviceman was, unfortunately, all too typical:

I went to a square dance in a neighboring town with some Indian and white friends. As I stood in line to get tickets, a policeman looked me over. He finally asked, "Are you Indian?" to which I proudly replied yes. He then said, "Well, you can't go in." I turned and walked away, followed by my friends who had joined me for an evening of fun. Although no one mentioned the incident as we drove back to Pembroke, it gave me a strange feeling. I couldn't help but wonder how I could be free everywhere except home.

Similarly, many Lumbees remember the shame they felt when the theater in Lumberton would allow Indians to sit only in the balcony. Although the theater is now integrated, some of these Lumbees still refuse to go into the building. The insistence of the Lumbee on democratic elections for Pembroke was just one manifestation of their renewed willingness to fight this kind of discrimination in Robeson County.

World War II changed Robeson County in other ways as well. Two major military installations—Laurinburg-Maxton Air Base and Fort Bragg—were established within 40 miles of Pembroke. Soldiers stationed there often came to the town on weekends, and some met and married Lumbee women. After the war, many Lumbee veterans also brought home non-Indian brides from all around the world. These intermarriages further helped to bring the Lumbee community out of its relative isolation. As had been the case with outsiders throughout their history, the Lumbee demonstrated a remarkable willingness to accept and assimilate these newcomers. This attitude has contributed in large part to the continued vitality of the Lumbee as a people.

The Lumbee community was affected by Indians moving away from Robeson County as well as by outsiders moving in. The postwar years were a time of significant northward migration by the South's minority populations, especially blacks. Hundreds of thousands of southern blacks left their homes for the automobile plants, steel mills, and manufacturing plants of the industrial north, where the hard times of the Great Depression of the 1930s had been succeeded by an economic boom brought about by World War II and the peacetime prosperity that followed. The war had forced the depressed U.S. economy to expand its productive capacity to the utmost, while the peacetime demands of the populace of the newly victorious nation for automobiles, washing machines, and other consumer goods, and of the government for weaponry and technology with which it could fulfill its newfound international responsibilities, ensured that the good economic times would continue. Thus, after the war, the nation's plants, mills, and factories needed manpower to keep them humming around the clock, and southern blacks went to the North in large numbers believing they would find not only greater economic opportunity there but a less overtly racist society in which, for example, legal segregation was unknown.

The Lumbee, too, were part of this trend. For America's farmers, the Great Depression had actually begun well before the stock market crash of 1929. Agriculture had enjoyed a boom during World War I, when war-torn Europe's demand for food had resulted in high export prices, but the return of peace to that continent in 1918 meant a crash for American agriculture that continued throughout the 1920s and 1930s. Like farmers across the United States, Lumbee farmers were hard hit; many lost their land, and it took several decades for agriculture in Robeson County to fully recover. Even when prosperity was restored in the 1940s, there was little economic opportunity in Robeson County for those Lumbees who did not wish to pursue farming as a livelihood.

(Although the availability of manufacturing and other jobs has increased significantly in the county since the 1940s, Robeson remains overwhelmingly agricultural and one of the poorest counties in North Carolina.) Consequently, starting in the late 1930s, Lumbees began to leave Robeson County in significant numbers to look for work in the nation's cities, with Baltimore and then Detroit (the center of the nation's automobile industry) being the most popular destinations. This trend accelerated after World War II, when many of those who left were returned servicemen, less reluctant, perhaps, as a result of their greater experience outside Robeson to leave the county. Today, Baltimore is home to a community of several thousand Lumbees.

As it was everywhere in the United States where legal segregation prevailed, the U.S. Supreme Court's decision in *Brown v. Board of Education of Topeka, Kansas* was a landmark event in the postwar history of Robeson County. In 1954, the Court ruled that segregation in public schools was inherently discriminatory and in so abolishing the prevailing doctrine of "separate but equal" laid the groundwork for the abolition of segregation in all public institutions and facilities. (The legal premise on which segregation was based was that it was not, for example, inherently discriminatory to mandate separate public schools for black and white children so long as the separate facilities were "equal." In most places, of course, any claim to equality in segregated fa-

The Brookses, a Lumbee family, in 1936. According to the anthropologist Karen Blu, "anyone attempting to identify racial affiliation in Robeson County solely on the basis of physical appearance is faced with an enormous variety . . . especially among Indians. Indians may vary in skin color from very light to quite dark. . . . Eye color ranges from blue to hazel to dark brown; hair texture from straight to wavy to very curly or even kinky; hair color from blond to brown to black."

cilities was nothing more than pretense. The greatest importance of the *Brown* decision was its decree that any segregation in public schooling, even if the facilities were in fact equal, was unconstitutional.)

The Lumbee's reaction to the Court's ruling was complex. Though obviously in favor of the dismantling of a legal system that defined them as second-class citizens, they worried that the Court's ruling would change the special character of the schools they had fought so hard to establish by allowing the admission of non-Indian students. At a time when few outsiders had been interested in the education of Lumbee children and young adults, the Lumbee had succeeded in establishing schools that addressed the unique needs of the children in their community; in the aftermath of the Supreme Court's ruling many Lumbee grew concerned that integration would result in the "de-Indianization" of their schools. Nevertheless, the Lumbee were quick to comply with the Court's decision. Pembroke State College had, in 1949, opened its doors to whites even before the *Brown* ruling was handed down—that there was any interest at all by white students in attending Pembroke is testimony to the quality of the education there, for

In the South, the gains made by the civil rights movement in the 1950s and 1960s resulted in a revival of white supremacist organizations such as the Ku Klux Klan, but the Lumbee prevented the Klan from making significant inroads in Robeson County.

as a rule, whites in the South did not want to attend nonwhite educational institutions—and after the decision Pembroke was one of the first southern colleges to abolish all racial restrictions. Today, Pembroke State University serves a racially mixed student body while maintaining its special relationship with the Lumbee people.

The Lumbee had similar concerns about the integration of their other educational institutions. While few of them insisted on maintaining all-Indian schools, the Lumbee have from the outset wished to ensure that the integrated public school system in Robeson County serves the special needs of its Indian students. Accordingly, the Lumbee have worked through the political system to modify the curriculum to provide for the teaching of Indian history and culture. In recent decades, the Lumbee have fought to exert a greater influence on the county school board—responsible for the appointment of teachers, the allocation of funds, and so on—where they have traditionally been underrepresented, with the result that, until recently, significant disparities in the allocation of funds and resources for schooling have continued to exist in Robeson County.

As the Supreme Court was taking the first steps toward the dismantling of the system of segregation under which the Lumbee were defined as second-class citizens, the Lumbee were taking measures of their own to assert their pride in their identity. The Reverend D. F. Lowry spearheaded a movement for state legislation officially recognizing the tribe by a designation other than the Cherokee Indians of Robeson County, the name by which the Lumbee had been known since 1913. Lowry and his followers suggested that their people be called the Lumbee Indians, because, as Lowry wrote in 1952, "the first white settlers found a large tribe of Indians living on the Lumbee River in what is now Robeson County—a mixture of colonial blood with Indian blood, not only of White's colony; but with other colonies following and with many tribes of Indians; hence, we haven't any right to be called any one of the various tribal names, but should take the geographical name, which is Lumbee Indians, because we were discovered on the Lumbee River." A referendum was held in 1953, and those Lumbees who voted—turnout was low—approved the new name by a 60 to 1 ratio. Though the choice of the name Lumbee did not end the anthropological controversy over their origins, or satisfy those members of the tribe who sought to identify themselves as descended from a single ancestral people, it did express who and what the Lumbee are: They are people of the river. Just as, for decades, they had made their homes on its banks, they found definition in its name. Three years after the referendum, the U.S. government, by way of an act of Congress, officially recognized the Lumbee by that name, though the legislation to that effect absolved the federal government of any responsibil-

Since the end of the Civil War, a burning cross has been the dreadful symbol used by the Ku Klux Klan to instill terror in blacks and other minorities.

ity to provide services or funds to the Lumbee similar to those it provided other recognized tribes.

Though in the aftermath of *Brown* and similar court decisions, white supremacists in Robeson County and its environs, as elsewhere in the South, were determined to maintain segregation, the Lumbee, as they had shown earlier in their history, were equally willing to fight for their freedoms and rights as American citizens. On January 13, 1958, the *Ku Klux Klan (KKK)*, a white supremacist organization, burned crosses on the front lawns of two Indian families in Robeson County.

When the Ku Klux Klan tried to hold a rally in an open field across the road from this pond outside Maxton, North Carolina, in January 1958, armed Lumbees broke up the gathering.

Since its founding in the immediate aftermath of the South's defeat in the Civil War, the KKK, in its various manifestations, has worked to terrorize minorities, particularly blacks. The organization had enjoyed a revival in the wake of the *Brown* decision and the beginning of the civil rights movement, with its members hoping that fear could be used as a tactic to prevent minorities from claiming rights to which they were entitled. The cross burnings in Robeson County were intended to send a threatening message to a Lumbee family that had recently moved into a white neigh-

borhood and to a young Lumbee woman who was supposedly dating a white man.

The KKK's actions in Robeson County in 1958 were orchestrated by James W. "Catfish" Cole, the "grand wizard" of a South Carolina branch of the Klan and a self-proclaimed advocate of segregation. Following the burnings, Cole announced that the KKK would hold a rally in Robeson County in order "to put the Indians in their place, to end race mixing." The Klan first tried to find a site near Pembroke for their meeting, No one was willing to rent them a location, so they finally decided to lease a field 10 miles away near the town of Maxton, where the rally was then scheduled for the night of January 18.

As word of the rally spread, Malcolm McLeod, the sheriff of Robeson County, paid Cole a visit. McLeod knew the Lumbee were angry and that they had no intention of allowing anyone to intimidate them in their own community. For the Klansmen's own safety, he advised the grand wizard to cancel the rally, but Cole chose to ignore the sheriff's warning; an organization in the business of sowing terror could not afford to be so easily run off, and the KKK did not really expect that anyone would stand up to them.

But at twilight on January 18, as the white-robed, white-hooded Klansmen began to gather on an open field near Hayes Pond outside Maxton, they discovered to their surprise that they were heavily outnumbered by Lumbee, many of whom were carrying firearms.

(The Klansmen were also armed.) Charles Craven, a reporter for the Raleigh *News and Observer*, described the scene this way:

> Darkness had descended. It was freezing cold. The cars kept coming. The Klansmen had set up headquarters in the center of the field. They had stretched a huge banner emblazoned with KKK and had erected a long pole with a naked light bulb on it. Religious music blared forth on the cold air from a public address system. The Indians were arriving in fours and sixes and were getting from their cars and lining the road. The armed Klansmen were at the little circle of cars in the center of the field and some patrolled at the edges of the darkness. Some of the young Indians along the road had begun laughing and shouting, giving war whoops. Now and again somebody would yell, "God Damn the Ku Klux Klan."

As several Lumbees tried to take down the single light that illuminated the field, a struggle broke out. A single shot blasted the lightbulb into shards, and in the sudden darkness gunfire sounded from all directions. In minutes, the highway patrol arrived to restore order. Though no one had been hurt, the Klansmen were frightened enough to welcome the intervention of the law. Escorted by the patrolmen, the routed KKK left the field to a chorus of derisive whoops and shouts from the Lumbee.

One Lumbee, Simeon Oxendine, the proprietor of a gas station in Pembroke and a decorated veteran of World War II, played a particularly important role in the confrontation. As he later recounted, "I helped to pull the Klan's flag down and this seemed to make them mad." Wrapped in the KKK's banner, Oxendine was photographed by journalists at the scene. When the rally became international news, the picture was reproduced in magazines and newspapers around the world. Hailed as a hero, Oxendine received thousands of letters, telegrams, and cablegrams. As its most famous participant, he summed up the significance of the Lumbee's fight against the KKK: "We killed the Klan once and for all. We did the right thing for all people."

To add to the KKK's humiliation, Catfish Cole and another Klansman, James Martin, were indicted for inciting a riot. The judge at Martin's trial was Lacy Maynor, a Lumbee. After announcing the defendant's conviction, Maynor told Martin, "You came into a community with guns, where there was a very happy and contented group of people. We don't go along with violence. . . . We can't understand why you want to come here and bring discord." Martin was ordered to serve 6 to 12 months in prison.

After being extradited from South Carolina, Cole was also tried and convicted. His sentence was imprisonment for between 18 to 24 months. Upon hearing the court's decision, Cole still showed no remorse for his actions. He told a reporter that "the action of the court in Robeson County had done more to prove in three and a half days than I have by my preaching in eight years that this country is fast falling into communism and dictatorship." Happily, his was a minority viewpoint, and the KKK has not returned to Robeson County since.

Following their rout of the Klan, the Lumbee began to devote an increasing amount of energy and attention to political activity as a means of securing a better way of life for themselves. Since the 1960s, an ever-increasing number of Lumbees have sought and won election to public office in Robeson County, on every level from local to state. Some have even won appointment to federal office.

At the same time, the debate over the true meaning of Lumbee identity has continued. In the 1970s, a relatively small group of Lumbee began to lobby for yet another reconsideration of the tribe's name. According to this faction, which organized itself as the Eastern Carolina Indian Organization (ECIO), the name Lumbee was largely devoid of historical or cultural significance; the group lobbied instead for federal recognition as Tuscarora Indians, an Iroquoian people resident in North Carolina prior to the 18th century, from whom they claimed the Lumbee had descended. The ECIO also advocated a return to all-Indian schools, feeling that in this way the Lumbee's Native American heritage could be better preserved.

Though the majority of Lumbee did not agree with the ECIO's views, the organization nevertheless had a profound influence, particularly after it gained the attention and support of the American Indian Movement (AIM), an activist group dedicated to calling attention to the United States's historical and ongoing mistreatment of its native peoples. AIM members, including national leaders Dennis Banks and Vernon Bellecourt, came to Robeson County to demonstrate with the Tuscarora on the school issue, and many of the Robeson County Tuscaroras traveled to Washington, D.C., to take part in the AIM protest known as the Trail of Broken Treaties, which brought Indians from dozens of different tribes all across the country to the nation's capital. Robeson County Tuscaroras were among the AIM members who occupied the Bureau of Indian Affairs building in Washington, and when the federal government determined to destroy AIM—an effort in which quasi- and extralegal tactics were employed—a number of Robeson County Tuscaroras were prosecuted for their alleged activities with AIM, though none were convicted. Though the Robeson County Tuscarora succeeded on neither the school nor the name issue, their activity forced the Lumbee to take a new look at their historical and cultural heritage, both as regards their identity as an individual people and the collective identity they share with all the native peoples of North America.

To many Lumbees, nothing was more symbolic of the identity they had built for themselves in Robeson County than the main building on the campus

A mural celebrating the Lumbee driving the Klan from Robeson County. In the foreground at center, in cap, is World War II hero Simeon Oxendine, who derisively draped himself in the KKK's flag.

of Pembroke State University. Old Main, as it was known, had been built in 1921; it was the last remaining edifice from the time when the school had served only Indians and as such was regarded by the Lumbee as a vital link to their past. Thus, the announcement in 1972 that the building was to be demolished to make way for a new auditorium aroused heated emotions in

Two members of the American Indian Movement (AIM) defend themselves in a federal courtroom. The militant tactics used by AIM to focus attention on the past and present mistreatment of Indian peoples made it the object of political persecution by the U.S. government.

the Lumbee community. Rallies were organized, petitions circulated, and funds raised, all for the purpose of saving Old Main. Many Lumbees took the position that the building belonged to them, as taxpayers, as much as it did to the state. (The state had originally provided the funds for Old Main's construction.) Others argued that for all Old Main's undeniable historical and cultural importance, the university—and by extension the Lumbee community—would be better served by a new building. The fight to save Old Main attracted nationwide attention; as Lewis Bruce, commissioner of the Bureau of Indian Affairs, put it: "Old Main is a monument to the Indian people throughout this country." Bruce's state-

ment reflected the recognized importance to all Native American peoples of the Lumbee's long fight for educational opportunity.

With the controversy over its preservation still unresolved, Old Main was torched by arsonists on March 18, 1973, and gutted by the ensuing fire. The culprits were never apprehended, but the near destruction of the building seemed to illustrate to all concerned just how tragic its complete loss would have been. Funds were made available for Pembroke State to acquire a new site for its auditorium; Old Main was restored and now houses the university's Department of American Indian Studies as well as a cultural center and museum.

Like any vibrant people's, the Lumbee's quest to define themselves, in terms of both their identity as a people and their relationship with the greater society, is ongoing. Many of the problems with which they have wrestled throughout much of their existence remain unresolved. Robeson remains one of the nation's poorest counties, and the Lumbee are, taken as a whole, some of its poorest citizens. Though well educated by the standards of other Native American peoples, the Lumbee are poorly educated in comparison with the American population as a whole. Though in recent decades Robeson has attracted more industry, the county remains predominantly rural, and economic opportunity there remains limited. Finally, non-Indian control of the political process at the state and county levels continues to adversely affect the

On March 18, 1973, a fire of suspicious origins gutted Old Main on the campus of Pembroke State University. The building had become the most prominent symbol of the Lumbee's educational and cultural achievements.

ability of the Lumbee to control matters of the greatest importance to their future as a people—the education of their children and the provision of services to the members of their tribe.

Yet, as they have throughout their history, the Lumbee continue to devise creative solutions to the problems that face them. Today, more Lumbee own their own land than at any time since the 1730s. Founded in Pembroke in 1971, Lumbee Bank is the first and oldest Indian-owned and -operated bank in the United States. The Lumbee newspaper, the *Carolina Indian Voice*, keeps its readers informed about events in Robeson County, especially those of significant interest to the Indian community. Its editorial objective, stated upon its founding by its editor, Bruce Barton, speaks to the aspirations of the Lumbee: "We hope . . . to turn discrimination and poverty and other related ills inside out by honest, objective reporting of happenings in Robeson County. We are proud of our Indianness but are not closeminded to the friendship of whites, blacks, or Indians of other areas. We feel cooperation is the key."

And the Lumbee continue to work through the political system to achieve an ever-increasing amount of self-determination. The 1988 campaign of Julian Pierce, a Lumbee, for the office of superior court judge illustrates the type of political issues with which the Lumbee remain concerned, their success in addressing them, and the work that remains to be done.

Pierce was a 42-year-old lawyer who had devoted the better part of his career to the establishment and direction of Lumbee River Legal Services, a clinic that provided legal advice and counsel to those too poor to afford a lawyer. Prior to the establishment of the clinic, the state and the county had made no provision for legal services for the indigent in Robeson. Pierce's campaign for superior court judge—a position that had never been held by a Lumbee—took place at a time of renewed racial tension in the county. Over white opposition, a coalition of black and Lumbee voters had approved a referendum providing for the unification of the county's five school districts, a measure the Lumbee had long supported in the belief that it would end the traditional disparity in the allocation of school funds between town and rural school districts, as well as that between schools in predominantly white localities and those in predominantly black or Indian communities. During this same time, the Lumbee had grown increasingly active in protesting what they regarded as a long-standing pattern of harassment, mistreatment, and brutality on the part of the Robeson County sheriff's department. An unarmed Lumbee had been shot to death by a sheriff's deputy in November 1986, and in early February 1988 two Lumbees took hostages at the offices of the *Robesonian* newspaper in Lumberton to protest continued police misconduct.

In this atmosphere, Pierce's campaign was seen to have great symbolic and practical importance; he said he was running because minorities in Robeson County received no respect from the criminal justice system. His opponent, the county district attorney, Joe Freeman Britt, was, to many, as great a symbol of minority discontent as Pierce was of hope for the future. Britt had won more death sentences than any other prosecutor in the country; a disproportionate number of those, charged his critics, had been given to black or Lumbee defendants.

On March 26, 1988, Pierce, who had received several death threats, was found murdered in his home. It was immediately speculated that he had been the victim of a political assassination, but subsequent investigation revealed that he had been shot as the outcome of a domestic dispute. The arrest of his killers did not lessen the tensions surrounding the election, however, for under state election law Pierce could not be replaced on the ballot, leaving Britt the automatic winner even though, as it turned out, the dead Pierce outpolled him in the April election. Such an outcome was extremely unsatisfactory to some of the Lumbee and black population of Robeson County, who successfully petitioned the governor, James G. Martin, for redress. Martin created another judicial post on the superior court and appointed Dexter Brooks, a Lumbee, to fill it. His decision was hailed as an enlightened first step toward creating a permanent climate of racial harmony and equality in Robeson County. For the

Julian Pierce, a Lumbee attorney, dedicated his career to providing legal services to the poor people of Robeson County. His 1988 campaign for Superior Court judge, which ended with his tragic murder and posthumous election to the position, focused attention on economic and social inequities in Robeson County.

blacks and Indians of the county, their joining together on the Pierce and school board consolidation issues offered an encouraging prospect for future cooperation toward the goal of attaining political representation more proportionate to their numbers in Robeson. (Together, the Lumbee and the blacks constitute a vast majority—63 percent—of the population of the county, but whites continue, as they have throughout Robeson's history, to

Lumbee actors perform Strike at the Wind, *a historical play about the life of Henry Berry Lowrie that is given annually as a celebration of the Lumbee heritage.*

exercise effective control of political office at the county level.)

In 1990, Adolph L. Dial, a Lumbee, was elected to the North Carolina General Assembly. The third Indian to serve in the General Assembly, Dial was appointed to the Redistricting Committee, whose job was to draw district lines for reapportionment after the 1990 census. In 1991, the North Carolina General Assembly approved the redistricting of Robeson County into three single-member districts for the North Carolina House of Representatives. One of those districts has a majority Indian population, thus assuring Indian representation for years to come.

The Lumbee dedication to education and political activity as a means of improving the lives of all their people bodes well for the future, but the surest indication of their future survival and even prosperity is their indomitable pride in their own cultural identity and the self-reliance they have demonstrated throughout their past. Their fight for full federal recognition and funds continues, spearheaded by the Lumbee Regional Development Association (LRDA), which functions as a kind of tribal coalition representing all the Lumbee of Robeson County as well as the smaller populations in adjoining Hoke County and the cities of Raleigh, North Carolina, and Baltimore, Maryland. Today, as throughout the Lumbee's history, there are those who would say that as the Lumbee do not fit any of the common definitions of Indianness, they are not really Indians. For such cultural skeptics, the Lumbee have a standard response. "My father and mother are Indians, my father's father and mother's mother were Indians, and their parents and grandparents were Indians. What else could I be?"▲

BIBLIOGRAPHY

Blu, Karen I. *The Lumbee Problem: The Making of an American Indian People.* New York: Cambridge University Press, 1980.

Bosco, Peter I. *Roanoke.* Brookfield, CT: Millbrook Press, 1992.

Dial, Adolph L. "Lumbee Indians." In *Indians of the Lower South: Past and Present.* Edited by John K. Mahon. Pensacola, FL: Gulf Coast History and Humanities Conference, 1975.

Dial, Adolph L., and David K. Eliades. *The Only Land I Know: A History of the Lumbee Indians.* San Francisco: Indian Historian Press, 1975.

————. "The Lumbee Indians of North Carolina and Pembroke State University." *Indian Historian* 4, no. 4 (Winter 1971): 20–24.

Evans, William McKee. *To Die Game.* Baton Rouge: Louisiana State University Press, 1971.

Harriott, Thomas. *A Briefe and True Report of the New Found Land of Virginia.* New York: Dodd, Mead, and Company, 1903.

Kupperman, Karen Ordahl. *Roanoke: The Abandoned Colony.* Totowa, NJ: Rowman and Allanheld, 1984.

GLOSSARY

blow fire A power that the Lumbee believed allowed its possessors to relieve the pain and blistering of burn victims with their hands and breath.

Bureau of Indian Affairs (BIA) A U.S. government agency now within the Department of the Interior. Originally intended to manage trade and other relations with Indians, the BIA today seeks to develop and implement programs that encourage Indians to manage their own affairs and to improve their educational opportunities and general social and economic well-being.

Burnt Swamp Association of the Mixed Race The Lumbee's first formal religious organization, formed by a group of Lumbee Baptists in 1880.

conjurers People who the Lumbee believed sold their souls to the devil in exchange for great mystical powers.

Croatoan The word found etched in a tree trunk at the site of the colony of Roanoke in 1591, the only evidence of the "lost" colonists who had arrived there four years before; it is believed to designate an island or region south of Roanoke inhabited by Indians friendly to the English settlers. Therefore, the Lumbee believe that they are the descendants of these lost colonists and the Indians with whom the latter merged; they were called the Croatan Indians until 1911.

cup readers Lumbees believed they possessed the ability to divine certain information by studying the signs left in the bottom of a coffee cup.

Great Depression The collapse of the U.S. economy in the 1930s, following the 1929 stock market crash.

Home Guard A combination militia-vigilante organization during the Civil War, made up of the white men of Robeson County who were not serving in the Confederate forces. This group had a reputation among the Lumbee for enforcing such land-grab schemes as the *tied-mule incidents*.

Indian Removal Act A bill passed by Congress in 1830. It authorized the president to set aside land west of the Mississippi River to which eastern tribes could be relocated, or removed. According to the terms of the act, no tribe could be removed against its will, although this provision was ignored in practice.

Ku Klux Klan An organization of southern white racists, originally founded in 1866 to terrorize nonwhites into not exercising the new legal rights given them during *Reconstruction*. In 1958, the Lumbee drove a modern incarnation of the Klan from Robeson County.

quitrents The practice of paying fees for the use of land in commutation of military service; part of the English system of land ownership by which North Carolina was surveyed and parceled out during the 18th century.

Reconstruction The era of social, political, and economic reorganization of the defeated South following the Civil War.

Roanoke Island Small island off the northeast coast of present-day North Carolina; site of the first English settlement in North America in 1585, which failed within 10 months. In 1587, a second group of colonists arrived at the island, only to vanish by the time supplies were brought from England. These "lost" colonists are thought to be the ancestors of the Lumbee Indians.

Robeson County The North Carolina county, located in the south-central part of the state along its border with South Carolina, that has been home to the Lumbee since the mid-17th century.

School Breaking The communal Lumbee celebration marking the end of the school year and the beginning of summer.

Scuffletown The name used by 19th-century whites to refer to Lumbee settlements or gatherings.

Slaughter Day A great feast, at which Lumbee family and friends gathered to kill hogs, prepare the year's supply of meat, eat heartily, and enjoy each other's company.

tied-mule incidents Episodes in which white farmers in Robeson County would bring their own livestock onto Lumbees' land and then inform the authorities that the Indians had stolen their animals. The Lumbees would often give the farmers some property in exchange for the dropping of the false charges.

tokens or **totens** Loud noises that the Lumbee believed were spirits announcing an impending death in the Indians' community.

tribe A society consisting of several or many separate communities united by kinship, culture, language, and other social institutions including clans, religious organizations, and warrior societies.

PICTURE CREDITS

AP/World Wide Photos, page 98; The Bettmann Archive, pages 17, 32, 46; Denver Public Library, Western History Department, page 94; Dr. Adolph L. Dial, pages 22, 33, 38, 42, 53, 56, 58, 60, 62, 64, 72, 73, 78, 80, 85, 95; Dr. Adolph L. Dial, Simeon Oxendine, and Shelby Woriax, page 93; Mrs. Lucy J. Harris, page 81; Courtesy Library of Congress, pages 15, 19, 26, 35; Maryland Historical Society, Baltimore, page 24; North Carolina Collection, University of N.C. Library at Chapel Hill, pages 14, 31, 40, 43, 44, 49, 51, 54, 61, 74, 76; Lloyd E. Oxendine, pages 73–80; Strike at the Wind! Theater, page 98; T/Sergeant William P. Revels, pages 12, 59, 68; T/Sergeant William P. Revels, Dr. Adolph M. Dial Collection, pages 20–21, 47, 70, 91; UPI/Bettmann, pages 83, 87, 88; Virginia State Library and Archives, page 28.

ADOLPH L. DIAL, a Lumbee Indian, is a professor at Pembroke State University in North Carolina, where he helped to establish the Department of American Indian Studies, which he now chairs.

In 1976, Dr. Dial was the recipient of the Henry Berry Lowry Award, the highest honor bestowed by the Lumbee community. He was also named Pembroke Kiwanian of the year for his work in community service and development. Among other distinctions he has received are an Honorary Doctor of Humane Letters degree from Greensboro College in 1985 and an honorary doctorate from Pembroke State University in 1988.

His publications include *The Only Land I Know: A History of the Lumbee Indians* (1975), which is recognized as the standard Lumbee history, and numerous articles on the Lumbee people.

FRANK W. PORTER III, general editor of INDIANS OF NORTH AMERICA, is director of the Chelsea House Foundation for American Indian Studies. He holds a B.A., M.A., and Ph.D. from the University of Maryland. He has done extensive research concerning the Indians of Maryland and Delaware and is the author of numerous articles on their history, archaeology, geography, and ethnography. He was formerly director of the Maryland Commission on Indian Affairs and American Indian Research and Resource Institute, Gettysburg, Pennsylvania, and he has received grants from the Delaware Humanities Forum, the Maryland Committee for the Humanities, the Ford Foundation, and the National Endowment for the Humanities, among others. Dr. Porter is the author of *The Bureau of Indian Affairs* in the Chelsea House KNOW YOUR GOVERNMENT series.